ABOUT THE AUTHOR

Nick Eynon is one of NZ t ...... become an author. He go. ... job or presenting *Destination Planet Earth* after constantly haranguing TV3 bosses for months via mail and phone calls, asking for work. Eventually, to get a night's peace, they agreed to give the boy a go.

Nick Eynon's

Destination Anywhere

Nick Eynon's

Destination Anywhere

Howling At The Moon Productions Ltd

First edition published 1998 (April) by
Howling At The Moon Productions Ltd
PO Box 302 188, North Harbour
Auckland 1310
New Zealand

ISBN 0-9583717-3-3
Typeset in Weiss

Cover concept by Heidi Robertson and Ian Wishart
Back cover photos by Nick Eynon and TV3, except Disneyland photos
of Candice Bergen, Robin Williams, John Goodman, Tom Selleck,
Jillie Mack and Bob Saget by Ian Wishart
Book design and layout by Graeme Leather, Island Bridge
Printed in New Zealand by Publishing Press Ltd

CONTENTS

FOREWORD | I remember the 17th of March 1997 like it was only yesterday. The crew of *Destination Planet Earth* stepped off a hot and exhausting long-haul flight from Hong Kong into the cool, fresh breeze of Auckland International Airport.

We had been travelling the global road for nearly six months, albeit with several short breaks, and circumnavigated sufficient distance to wind ourselves four times around the earth, visited ten countries and shot over 160 beta tapes of footage. Physically and mentally, the crew was spent, and the idea of boarding another overseas flight had less appeal than a long and painful death.

For almost five months after my return, people had often asked:

'Off around the world again?' or

'Must be due for another passport, Nick?'

The idea, at first, was absurd. I was in the working depths of a doomed game show and was aware that TV3 had no immediate plans to launch a second series for at least some time. Or so I thought.

No matter how many miles endured, journeys made or rubbery economy meals consumed, travel has held an almost endemic fascination with New Zealanders and, despite the debilitating shooting schedules and vast distances, I would be lying if I said I didn't experience any pleasure from it. So when the inevitable phone call arrived from the Executive Producer asking me to pack my bags, I proceeded to do the most logical thing that the situation called for. I packed my bags.

If the promotions department had a problem in naming the show, I could suggest several alternatives – *The Longest Way Around The World* or *The Luxuries of Aerial Transport* would be two of the most obvious. Despite most of the journey being made on aircraft, we completed the gaps on a wide range of transport including van, minibus, Vespa, motorbike, hydro-foil, rollerblades, tuk-tuks, trams and horse-drawn carts.

The bulk of the journey was made between January 1997 and January 1998. We filmed for 136 days, passed through over 21 countries and stayed in more than 30 hotels. An average day involves a large amount of travel and preparation for filming, so I have kept the 'technical jargon' to a minimum, and included many of the lighter moments that people will never see on screen. It should be noted the order of the countries visited differs considerably from the order of shows in the finished television production.

The period between the start and end of filming was indeed an exceptional one. Many of the countries we visited had undergone, or were undergoing, momentous changes. Our visit took us through Hong Kong, which was now under Chinese political rule, and we had front row seats when Scotland cast its favorable Independent Parliament vote. Macau was experiencing its most turbulent Mafia violence in over 20 years and, as the deaths of Diana, Princess of Wales and Mother Teresa were sending shock waves around the world, we were already knee deep in flowers outside Kensington Palace. The Paris Metro was bombed only a few days before our arrival, Belfast witnessed three murders during our stay, and a lone assassin gunned down an innocent tourist at the Empire State Building during the research week in New York.

This book is based upon the diaries and recordings kept at the time of my journey. I have done my best to describe the pain and pleasure, the rewards and setbacks of a television crew putting together a prime time network show 'on the road'. I have deliberately kept the notes and entries untouched since my return, to keep the story in its most raw and uncut form.

During the few opportunities that I had to record information, I took the liberty of noting a number of interesting statistics that enforces the magnitude of our travels:

Total number of kilometres travelled	301,500 km
Kilometres travelled by air	282,894 km
Cruising altitude	30,000 ft
Altitude when I sky-dived out of a plane in Africa	10,000 ft
Weight of gear taken to New York by crew	325 kg
Time spent in the air	323 hours
US dollars paid to Balinese custom as a bribe to let our camera pass through immigration	300
Polaroid photographs taken during all TV shoots	296
beta tapes used by cameramen in the production	210

In-flight movies available to the crew to watch	136
Hours spent in departure and transit lounges	102
Meals eaten on planes by crew members	99
Anti-malaria tablets consumed during the African-Asian shows	78
Inspections of baggage by customs officials	55
Countries visited during the shoot	21
AA batteries used in my Walkman during flights	20
Number of times I had to jump off a bungy-tower	15
Average number of bags and cases taken by crew on trips	14
Different modes of transport used	10
Number of times I was sunburnt	8
Number of flights spent in economy class	7
Average hours of sleep per night while overseas	6
Number of hotels used in the 8 day Zimbabwe shoot	5
Number of rainy days encountered on travel	4
Lost items	2
Number of empty pages in my passport	1

What you read is what we experienced in those extraordinary months between August and January – blood, sweat, tears and all that.

Not every single day on the trip has been transcribed. Rest days when nothing happened except laundry and sleeping have been omitted out of consideration for the reader. There is a general rule that 'what goes on tour, stays on tour'. I have preserved the credibility and privacy of individuals, organisations and incidents that the author felt inappropriate to this text. (That should keep you guessing!)

Staunch followers of the television series will notice the absence of several destinations. This is due to a lack of comprehensive diary notes. The cities of London, Rome, Dublin and Hong Kong – though covered on the show – do not feature in this production.

Nick Eynon, Wellington 1998

THE CREW *Cathay Pacific Destination Planet Earth* was in every sense, a team effort. Steve Orsbourn, Jim Henderson, Tim Pattinson, Cameron McGrath, Matt Heine, Tony Wilson and Paul Dodge travelled with me almost everywhere and I owe them enormous and almost inexpressible thanks for not only being the best technicians in the business but for being the very best travelling companions. Similar gratitude to Peta Carey, Matt Sumich, Justin Cockerill and the superb collection of directors Nigel Carpenter, Mark Everton and Rob MacLaughlin who all injected their own exceptional styles into the series, and taught me countless invaluable lessons on the way. I consider them all as great friends as well as work colleagues.

I also had the honour of working with some of the most famous faces in New Zealand television who provided a fresh breath of air for each destination. Thanks to Theresa Healey, Anita McNaught, Jools and Linda Topp, Lynette Forday, Jennifer Weather-Centre, Mary Lose, Louise Wallace, Rachel Hunter, Petra Bagust, Leanne Malcolm, and the dynamic duo of Kerre Woodham and Belinda Todd who gave a young inexperienced presenter a priceless introduction to the world of television.

ACKNOWLEDGEMENTS Like any television production, its success lies in the supreme collective effort of a number of people at different levels. I have done my best to name as many of those technicians, officials and executives as possible, and any name overlooked is due to my failure to recall as opposed to any lack of commitment on their part.

The two most important people to thank are Darryl McEwen and Bettina Hollings who both took an enormous gamble on selecting an inexperienced presenter for such a high profile programme. I hope I have been able to repay their considerable faith with my performances in the show. Also much gratitude to Louise Hudson and the Cathay Pacific team, together with Budget Travel who both fulfilled the professional sponsor role.

The research team of Clare Barker, Coral Barrett, Jude Callen, Dave Collins and Tania Styles for shouldering the brunt of preparation work, Josie Ward, Cindy Lucas and Ross Peebles for providing continuity, and thanks also to the tireless team of editors and technicians who played an equally important role in the finished product – especially Phil Englund and the irrepressible Scott Flyger who was responsible for the majority of Series Two editing. A fine effort.

Paul Dodge and Dave Collins were responsible for the production and organisation for the first and second series respectively. The high quality levels and subsequent top ratings were due largely to the tireless labour of these two individuals. There is no understating the fact that a project of this magnitude becomes so self-consuming that their lives revolved around it, and for the last 14 months Paul and Dave have lived and breathed 'DPE' more than anyone else. Top job, fellas.

Chapter 1 | Indonesia

Day 1, Monday 13th January

My alarm wakes me at 2pm but my digital watch is still on New Zealand time so I'm not really sure what day it is. After confirmation from the hostess that it is Monday, I also discover that we are 3 hours from our destination. Sometimes I question the merits of sleeping on the plane. I feel dog rough. Belinda Todd, my co-host for this shoot, is sleeping soundly.

After slipping into another restless fit of dozing, I'm woken by what sounds like a faulty, choking vacuum cleaner. The noise, however, is coming out of cameraman Steve Orsbourn's nostrils. I give up the notion of sleeping, in exchange for a documentary on John McEnroe that is screening on my personal TV. The wheels of Flight CX789 scorch into the sweltering tarmac of Denpasar Airport at exactly 8.45pm – right on time.

Sadly, the Indonesian customs aren't so punctual. Armed with 21 pieces of luggage, we are kept waiting for 45 minutes before the airport adviser acknowledges our existence. Several uniformed officials poke at the gear before mumbling something incomprehensible to each other. The whole charade is unravelling into a scene from *Dad's Army* whereby a whole squadron of Indonesian custom officers display their ineptitude with a fine performance of 'foot shuffling' and 'head scratching'. Eventually, it becomes obvious that we need to pay a 'backhander' in order to get the camera past customs . . . US$300.

Our producer Paul Dodge is furious.

'We're making a show about people coming here, for goodness sake! We could turn around and go home!'

Blank looks from officers.

'They're quite used to this' I whisper to Steve.

'God, I bet they make a fortune'

We have spent the next hour waiting in 34 degree heat, only to have to pay a bribe. Not the warmest of welcomes for a TV crew. The first impression at any airport is a lasting one, and this one sucks. A bunch of beady-eyed bureaucrats clearly taking the piss out of foreigners does not sit well with any of us.

'This is the kind of underhand tactics used by officials in this part of the world'

The comment comes from Richard Blanchette, the Club Med representative who is travelling with us. He explains that no-one escapes the constant haranguing for money, and warns us that there will be plenty more to come. Given that I am the most tight-fisted individual in the industry, his warning is wasted on me.

Denpasar is the largest city on the island of Bali but is not our major destination which takes the form of Nusa Dua beach – 16 kilometres south of our hotel. The minibus trip takes roughly 20 minutes and, although the island is already shrouded in darkness and a thick mist, it takes on a more tropical and considerably cleaner look than Hong Kong. And it doesn't stink of eggs. I talk to our guide, Manik, about the island. He is passionate about Bali and the emphasis placed on its tourism.

'The government have put a lot of money into the industry' he says. 'The roads and parks have been upgraded significantly. Our highways are the best and cleanest in the world.'

He's right. For some curious reason, the roads are impeccably kept. We are surrounded by the most desolate and impoverished landscape, yet the highways looked swept and hosed.

'Bali has plenty to offer' he continues.

'It is real resort, full of fun and culture, adventure and scenery.'

He sells well. However he conveys, with some sadness, that the quality of life for the average Balinese is poor compared with the rest of Indonesia. The cost of living is low but the average Balinese wage is, relatively speaking, insufficient.

Arriving at Club Med, we are ceremoniously greeted by a waving, clapping consortium of hotel staff who are either rolling drunk or unhealthily enthusiastic for this time of night.

'Hello, hello, hello.'

'Welcome Noo Zeeland!'

'Hey man. Get your party pants on.'

I wish they would shut up. I just want my room and a shower.

Before I get the chance to punch someone's lights out or carry off a native girl, I am thrust a room key and a tropical drink – which looks like bath water but tastes pleasantly like pear juice – and help the crew unload the equipment.

The rooms are have fantastic air-conditioning and it coolly wafts onto my sweaty body as I unpack my crumpled clothes. Peta Carey, our director for the week, calls in to go over the schedule. She is tanned and refreshed, and promises an action-packed week. I nod wearily at her enthusiasm. A huge spider dangles gingerly from the light in my dunny, and prompts a Babe Ruth performance with my towel to get rid of it.

Showered and changed I settle into bed and pop my anti-malaria pills. I have been taking the pills for a couple of weeks prior to my departure and they continue to taste like sweat socks. As soon as my head hits the pillow, I'm asleep and dreaming of native women . . . chasing me. I am running but going nowhere.

The first light of day breaks in the sky and, as I wearily peer out my window, it immediately reveals what could only be described as an outdoor adventurer's playground – swimming pools, sports activities, and gymnasiums. Because we arrived at 10.30pm last night, the entire complex was swamped in darkness.

After a quick breakfast with the crew, we're ready to shoot and the schedule starts with a series of multi-sports that Club Med provides. I jump into a professional tennis lesson and provide adequate evidence why a Maori may never win Wimbledon, blasting four first serves into the turf only a few metres in front of me. I'm not a bad tennis player, really. I happen to be bollocks today.

After a cool, sharp exit, archery beckons as the next challenge.

I complain to Dodgy that I am distracted by the fact that my instructor happens to be a 21 year old Brazilian beauty called Malina. I am beginning to get cramps in my side from sucking-in my stomach. I pursue with my arrow-shooting skills – almost eliminating the local wildlife nearby in the process – and then shoot a bull's eye a few seconds after the camera is turned off. Typical.

Trapeze swinging, swimming and a weights workout are added to our schedule and, judging by the underarm patches of sweat, it's safe to say that the DPE crew will make full use of the Club's pool facilities. The heat is oppressive and quickly drains the energy from all of us.

Into the minibus and onto the famous Kuta Beach which lies on the Western side of the island, and is home to something distinctly 'kiwi' – A.J. Hackett's Bungy Jump, a towering structure that has been purpose built for 'adrenalin junkies' who hang by elastic bands. I have a chat with Glenn – an Aussie who heads the operation – about living and working in Kuta. I have to admit that I am a poor listener (at the best of times) and everything he says is mixed into an indistinguishable blur as I peer over the edge in anticipation. I feel increasingly queasy as I prepare for the jump.

It's great fun – everything I expected – and a second jump is required for different camera shots. It's a real head rush to do it yourself and, alternatively, you can always stand on the ground and watch others, perhaps your wife or girlfriend, do it – one of the few chances you'll have in life to see her screaming and throwing up with her skirt around her head. Unless she's a 'scarfie' in which case any Saturday night at the pub should do the trick.

Kuta is the place where everybody seems to stay, and many never leave. In the 60's, it was one of the Big K's – Kathmandu, Kabul and Kuta. The main attraction, apart from the beachfront, is the shopping.

Belinda has the opportunity to test that theory, while I set up camp on the beach to shoot a few swimming and body-boarding sequences in the breaking surf. The first thing you notice about Bali is the tourism. It's in your face and ever present, and nowhere more prominent than on the beaches. The locals have grabbed hold of the great potential dollar and in these spots they're there to sell, sell, sell. If you show any weakness, they will hassle you relentlessly. Dodge is a prime target:

'Please sir, this a very fine necklace,' they plead.

Dodge's reply is firm. 'No.'

'Please sir, I will drop the price, drop it lower.'

'No.'

'Sir, best quality. Cheap for your wife.'

'Okay, but just one.'

This is the wrong reply. As soon as the transaction is made, there is a massive surge of sellers towards my producer. In the end, you have to be rude and coarse. If you don't, then you become a sitting duck. My replies are blunt:

'And you, sir?'

'Not a chance.'

'But you like a watch, yes?'

'I've got one, chief. What do I want another one for?'

'Very cheap, very cheap.'

'I have NO money.'

'Then why are you so happy?'

It's Balinese pizza for dinner at Kuta Centre and, after a day of such adventure, there is an added bonus in the form of a Kuta Beach sunset. After the sun drops in an orange afterglow, it intensifies and dies like the ember of a dying fire – either that or I've been smoking something a little thicker than a Camel cigar. Instead of showering, I opt for a swim courtesy of the Club Med pool.

We all congregate on the plastic deck chairs, listening to the multitude of '18-30ers' chanting and singing their way through a game of 'marshmallow volleyball' (Don't ask!)

We sit in silence, sipping slowly on the bar beverages, happy to be resting our legs for the first time in 24 hours.

Our sound man 'Lucky' Jim Henderson is eating local bacon for breakfast but I'm not so brave and decide on Western Muesli. The whole vibe of Club Med is generally 'western' in an Asian backdrop. No time for real reflection, however, as we head off. The weather feels distinctly tropical, hot and humid, still and muggy. Combined with the winding roads and fresh rain that is falling, the scenery seems to be getting better the further inland we drive.

It's craft-time, and we pull into Singapadu Gallery and are met by an array of stone and metal carvers who are knee deep in their work. The gallery sells jewellery in the form of some rather intricate and expensive craftsmanship – a necklace running into close to NZ$5,000 catches the eye but not my wallet.

Onto the town of Ubud, in which we split up to cover separate stories. Belinda is lucky enough to meet Don Antonio Blanco, a rather eccentric Spanish artist who has sold paintings to a number of famous celebrities including Michael Jackson. He can only be described as a geriatric eccentric self-promoter, in my view, but he's marvellous TV talent!

'The bosom of the woman is a beautiful thing,' he laughs. 'You can find many attractive Asian bosoms in my art.'

Right, I'll take the lot then.

I draw the comparative short straw in Mr. I Ketut Soki, another original artist but, to me, of less calibre. His style is more 'cartoony' than classical, but is still impressive. His offer of drinks has to be politely refused as we are running behind schedule.

The Barong Dance, held at Batubulan, is a small performance by a number of local artists who, dressed in traditional costume, act out the legendary story of Rangda (a mythological monster) and Barong (a mythological animal) who represent an eternal fight between good and evil. The series of choreographed acts culminate in the eminent death of the monster. Apart from Steve, who has to operate the camera, we all appreciate the cultural injection and follow it up with a fleeting visit to the Bird Zoo and Losman accommodation areas.

After an over-ride of craft and culture, I'm ready for some serious water sports – which Peta Carey (this week's director) provides by insisting we go white water rafting at Sobek Bina Utama on the River Ayung. With a microphone sellotaped to my hairless chest and the safety

Belinda Todd and Nick Eynon (partially obscured) on the River Ayung.

DESTINATION ANYWHERE

helmet firmly covering my nut, we set off. The river flow looks like the remains of a flushed toilet but we are assured that it's safe. The trip takes one-and-a-half hours and we are well looked after by our intrepid and cheerful guides 'Co-Co Pop' and 'Bello' (not their real names!)

'Nothing in this river to worry about. Only crocodiles and snakes,' they giggle.

'Thanks boys. I think I'll skip on the swim.'

Seconds later, I am neck-deep in murky river water. Bastards.

The day comes to a finish with a traditional Indonesian feast of dead and dried things – it's times like these that I would die for a Big Mac – but because it took our hosts almost 12 hours to prepare, I am grateful. Ketut cooks the meal, with members of his family helping to peel the vegetables and skin the meat. Some of the chicken and rice is divine, but there is an earthy smell to the fried duck, which doesn't appeal.

My offer to wash the dishes is refused, together with a confused look from our host, as I realise the meal has been served on leaves. I offer to rake the dishes.

The High Cliffs and the Uluwatu Temple make a pleasant start to the day, both are significant tourist traps but are deserted when we arrive. Religion dominates the lives of these people and because the Bali population are predominantly Hindu, the numerous temples are well preserved and beautifully attended. The Uluwatu temple dates back to 1100 AD, the oldest in Bali, whose ornate and intricate carvings are seen on many houses around this area.

The three Hindu Gods are depicted in stone on the open face of the temple, Brahma (The God of Fire and Creation – represented inside the temple by incense sticks), Vishnu (God of Water – represented by the holy water) and finally, Shiva (God of Air and Destruction – exemplified through flower offerings).

Following the brief shoot, we take a few photographs of the cliff monkeys – permanent residents around these parts. They are disobedient creatures and Peta almost loses her glasses in a speedy swipe from a hairy arm; the constant influx of tourists prompts an arrogance in their behaviour and they can be particularly nasty around children. The High Cliffs protrude from the otherwise barren landscape and fall dramatically to an angry ocean. Peta had spoken of the harsh beauty of the Cliffs but seeing is believing. The rain starts to fall, prompting the crew is scarper beneath a stone shelter. The shower has caused the temperature to drop significantly. Manik and his crew wait patiently by the van for our return:

'You guys are so vigilant.' I notice they have been waiting for well over 3 hours.

'No, Nick. It's in our nature.' he replies.

'Well, you should give me some of your nature.'

The remainder of the day is spent travelling inland to Mount Batu, with a fleeting visit to the surrounding villages. The lack of modern conveniences (like water!) provides a relaxed and relatively simple life for the people in this area, and it makes us contemplate our own seemingly attractive existence. The males of the village gather in groups to play mahjong and cards, while the women carry heavy baskets of produce up and down the mountain – no real change there.

Dodgy hires a motorbike that Belinda and I use to negotiate the tricky mountain roads, while Steve films for pleasure. We head further uphill to view the rice paddies and the irrigation systems that were built as far back as 1000 years ago. The landscape is dotted with the fine lines of rice

On the slopes of Mt Batu, Bali.

stems, farmers tending their pasture and duck shepherds. We park on the shores of Lake Bratan and paddle an old fishing dingy through the murky depths of the volcanic lake. On a fine day, the staggering backdrop of three volcanoes can be seen but the mist and low cloud spoils the chance for a classic shot. The peaceful and tranquil setting must be a popular destination for tourists but our guide reveals that it is the holiday haunt for the local Indonesians. We pass a village dairy that sells Coke and Cheezels, and present our collections to the crew on our return. Jim looks suspiciously at his bag of munchies:

'What?' I ask.

'I ordered Salt 'N' Vinegar.'

'The shop sold tiger penises. Do you really think they have a huge selection of crisps?'

Jim eats his Cheezels.

Night falls as we travel back to Nusa Dua, and has fallen by the time we arrive.

I'm woken at 5.00am by the sound of mowing machines. Not one or two but a whole squadron of them, unleashed on the grass surrounding my villa in an impressive display of formation lawn mowing. Despite the early call, I sit on the verandah to watch the performance and applaud madly at its conclusion.

We need to catch an early plane out to Lombok Island – a 20 minute flight away – so it is a frantic rush to load our gear into the van. Lombok is regarded by many travel hounds as the 'best kept secret' when concerning Indonesian holiday destinations. The island boasts some outstanding tropical scenery, dotted with ancient temples and very few tourists. It's a real getaway option, the way Bali used to be.

The day is warm but humid, so mineral water and insect repellent are used in abundance. We have a new driver, Miasa, who is accompanied by a gang of helpers, who all contribute to a lively atmosphere when we arrive. He explains that the average Lombok native is more relaxed and easy-going than the Bali equivalent and their good nature provides many laughs as the van ploughs its way through the palm trees and rice fields.

'We have more fun than those guys!'

'Yeah, we can pretty wild sometimes too!'

'How?'

'Steve can drink beer through his nose.'

Jim and some friendly monkeys, Lombok.

'Eeeeerrrghhh!' they all shout.

We climb approximately 400 stone steps up to the top of Pensong Temple for a general view of the island. There is a cluster of friendly monkeys awaiting our arrival, and they gaze knowingly as we explore their territory. The temple monument has one distinguishing feature – a reversed Nazi swastika – emblazoned on the front gate. This is not a symbol of Hitler's uprising but of Balinese culture; meaning life and unity. The Germans stole it for their own use.

Peta has planned a full day which starts with a ride on a horse drawn cart called a Cidomo, a wander through the paddy fields and a shopping visit to a local village potter. We encounter scores of young girls who attempt to sell their wares – which include clay animal statues, china plates and bead necklaces. The prices are exceedingly low, but the problem lies in the transaction. Once you buy from one trader, you become easy prey for the rest. Dodge doesn't want a similar experience to Kuta Beach.

Lombok Beach is, by contrast to Kuta, clean and unblemished. Instead of sand, the beach is made up of tiny pebbles that tickle your feet when you run across its golden floor. Although it takes several hours to reach, the rewards lie in its remote location and exquisite beauty.

We bump into a Kiwi girl who is working as a surfing instructor. She loves Lombok and makes a point of emphasising its numerous advantages over the main island. We wash the sand from our feet and begin the lengthy trek home.

Our accommodation for the night is the Sheraton Hotel, a 5-star top of the range facility. Sadly, due to the nature of our hectic schedule we arrive in the dark and only use it as a place to rest our weary heads.

'Ah, yes, hello. Room service? I want a pizza. I don't care, just throw everything on.'

I demolish my gourmet meal and watch CNN. World news update keeps me in tune with what's going on in the world.

DESTINATION ANYWHERE

The final day of the shoot is gearing up to be the best. Several boat trips and a sunset meal are on the agenda. I prepare myself by spending an hour in the hotel Fitness Suite. I am observed by several of the gym staff, whose quizzical looks indicate that not many guests workout at 7.30am in the morning. The suite is empty and eventually their curiosity leads me into conversation. Sugu and his friends are interested in knowing about New Zealand, so I don my ambassador hat and give them the full rundown . . . beer, racing, rugby et al. Similarly, they convey the difficulty in forging a living in this part of Asia. Life is hard by Western standards due mainly to the combination of a massive population and lack of disposable income. Although most children seek an education, for some it is too much of a financial struggle.

They tell me of the hardship that besets the majority of Indonesians, heightened by bad hygiene, adverse weather conditions, lack of quality and profitable employment but are also quick to emphasise the lack of class extremities – less rich, less poor. My biceps may be suffering from lack of stimulation but I have gained a mind of information.

After a room service breakfast, we catch a small fishing vessel at Pemenang for the 30 minute trip to the Gilli Isles. The Gillis are made up of three separate islands, all sparsely populated and bordered with fine white sand which extenuates the raw elegance of this 'pocket paradise'.

We are luck enough to discover the pleasures of Gilli Aik, complete with coral reef and schools of tropical fish. Armed with a snorkel and mask, Belinda and I explore the depths while above water the boys use the boat as a diving board.

Unfortunately, a few drops of water have appeared in the underwater camera casing causing a premature end to filming. Nevertheless I continue to play underwater and experience the beauty of a foreign reef.

Numerous brightly coloured fish pass between my fingers as I attempt to acquaint myself. The sun burns brightly

"Cambo", South East Asia "vet" Steve Orsbourne, ready to shoot, Club Med.

on the tropical shore as we wander into a quiet village for a cool drink, Jim and Steve have turned pink but aren't worried – a small price to pay for a day in paradise.

Our time is almost up so we board the boat and return to Miasa and the team who are waiting at Pemenang. The trip back to the main island is aboard a large jetfoil vessel that sways its way through the rocky ocean. Dodge and Steve have discovered a new sport, 'surfing on the roof of a hydrofoil', their antics take a chunk out of my cameraman's leg.

To our surprise we catch the tail end of dinner – a mixture of mince meat, noodles, sauce – and retire to our quarters to pack the bags. There are quite a few fresh faces around the club which indicates a number of departures and new batch of arrivals. My body aches from the outdoor activity and my neck is tingling from the sunburn...but what a day!

CHAPTER 2 | THAILAND

Day 7, Sunday 19th January

This morning is the first opportunity I have had to look around Club Med. I buy some photographs at the souvenir shop before taking a handful of photos at the beach and then grab a light breakfast at the Bar. The humidity continues to drain my energy, and by the time I have returned to my room I am coated in sweat.

After another shower, it is time to depart. A quick farewell to the staff – who have hardly seen us at all this week – and exchange of pleasantries with Manik and his team at the airport, before passing through customs (with a wary eye!) and on board Flight CX789.

I have fallen asleep during the flight with my television headset wrapped around my head and have managed to almost choke myself. This is our first day off for a week but it's hardly relaxing due to the heavy flight schedule that we have been given. Due to a sponsorship deal, we must fly to all destinations via Hong Kong so our flight paths are bizarre to say the least. Instead of flying direct to Bangkok, we must travel an additional 8 hours to and from Kai Tak International.

'This is crazy. Absolutely crazy' I say to Belinda. She's asleep.

It was with heavy hearts that we left Bali, but the nature of the shoot forced us to look ahead as our attention turned to the Asian metropolis of Bangkok – leaving Indonesia as a distant memory.

On route to Bangkok we dropped two of our party – Richard, who returned to a toasty summer in New Zealand and a normal life in Auckland and Peta, who was preparing to brave a research week in India. As soon as the landing gear touched tarmac, we were engulfed in a blanket of thick, hot air that is typical for this part of the continent. The airport and customs lounge was remarkably clean, quick and efficient as we passed from airport limbo to bona fide tourists.

It is difficult to dispel the images that Bangkok airport conjures up in the mind of any innocent tourist. The publicity surrounding individuals who have been caught in the act of 'drug trafficking' in these parts gives rise to cautious looks when you enter the immigration depot, but it all proves to be pointless as we stroll merrily through with 18 pieces of television luggage.

I am often stopped by airport officials and questioned comprehensively, even when my colleagues are completely ignored. Today is no different. Two uniformed guards question my nationality and check my passport:

'Where are you going?'

I have rehearsed my reply.

'We're filming a travel show for New Zealand television.'

'You bring alcohol, tobacco?'

'No.'

Steve shouts from beyond the check point: 'He's got an Uzi up his arse!'

The others wait, and then we wander into the arrivals lounge and are met by Mark Everton, our new director, who is flanked by two Thailand representatives. Kris is a middle-aged guide who works for the tourist company that also supplies us with a driver and a minibus. Pop (not his real name) is an officer from the Thailand Tourist Board, whose job is to get us into religious and various restricted areas without causing any major diplomatic incidents. Both are incredibly enthusiastic that we are filming a travel documentary about their city, and their energy has obviously had an influence on Mark – who can't stop talking about the magnificence of Bangkok.

'Guys, this city is amazing. Just amazing. You're gonna love it!'

'Has it got a gym?' I enquire, ignoring his references to some of the most breathtaking scenery this side of the globe.

'Oh yeah, and an awesome restaurant.'

'Do we have to pay?'

'Course you have to pay!'

That's all I really seem to hear as I gaze out into the Thailand evening. The weather is stuffy and close but the air conditioning unit keeps us cool and comfortable. Kris gives a quick summary of the week's activities before I fall into a sleepy doze. Next thing I know I'm unlocking the door to Room 1902 in the Grand China Princess Hotel – our home for the next 6 days. The hotel, like most in Bangkok, has a wealth of facilities ranging from breakfast bar, restaurant and indoor shopping malls to fitness centres and underground bank.

The staff are all dressing in impeccably clean turquoise uniforms, an image reinforcing the Thai's professional and demanding work ethic. One problem we will not have is lack of service or co-operation. From only a few hours in this country, it becomes glaringly obvious that these people have a laid back and compatible approach to life. No problem seems to be too big or small for them to handle. Any concierge's patience would be put to the test if a television crew dumped a mountain of equipment cases on his doorstep, but all we get in return is a few healthy smiles and a swarm of porters transporting luggage upstairs.

'Which room, sir?'

'Um, 2140.'

'Which cases, sir?'

'All of them please.'

'But there are 15 cases, sir.'

'I know.'

'You must have lots of socks, sir.'

Steve has to organise his 15 cases of camera and tape equipment before tomorrow. While bedtime is called around 11.00pm, Steve won't rest his head until 1.00am.

I return to my room and drink both of the complimentary bottles of mineral water supplied by the hotel. We are warned that the daytime temperature will exceed the early thirties tomorrow – so we hydrate ourselves in preparation for the deadly heat.

It is not a common occurrence, while travelling, that I am given the opportunity to exercise while on location. The limits on your time are often restricting enough to allow you only three 'excesses': food, sleep and headaches. This general rule is put to the test, however, if you can manage to swindle a hotel that has a fitness centre. And, on the 6th floor of the Grand China Princess, there lies the latest in exercise technology.

It proves to be a welcome respite and a chance to sweat out those evil travel toxins. The view of Bangkok from my stair-climber proves to be an added bonus. It really is magnificent, though shrouded in mist and smog – like most Asian cities. The landscape is rugged and modern but tends more to conjure up images of Ridley Scott's Blade Runner rather than the romantic efforts of travel writers.

After getting a grip on my workout, I decide its time to earn my crust, and hit the road. Our call time this morning is 6.00am and despite the fact that I have been up for 2 hours I feel quite refreshed. I meet up with the crew in the foyer, Kris and Pop are forever smiling while Jim, Ors and Dodge harp on about the fantastic meal they were served last night. Anything to get me out on the beers.

'Do you think this is okay to wear today?' Belinda asks Kris.

She is wearing open-toed heels, which are not permitted inside temple walls.

Kris gives a concerned look.

'I think that we had better be safe than sorry' she quips and rushes to change.

I have anticipated these cultural restrictions and am decked out in slacks and long-sleeved shirt. Within minutes the sweat pools at the base of my spine and runs down my leg. Politically correct clothing, but incredibly impractical in this weather.

We join the rat race in our mini-bus and head towards the first major tourist attraction for the day, the Grand Palace – home of the Emerald Buddha. Its only a 15 minute drive from the hotel and we have been advised to acknowledge the traditional customs of temple etiquette – which involves correct dress...long trousers or long skirt, shoes but no sandals or sneakers, shirt with long sleeves.

With dress in full respectability, Belinda and I enter the Palace with cameras discreetly rolling. The Palace gets progressively busier throughout the morning but it does our cause a lot of good, providing adequate backdrop to our needs. A busy place looks like a popular place on film. The Grand Palace covers an area of approximately 218,000 square metres and is surrounded by walls that were originally built in 1783. The length of the four walls totals 1900 metres (you wouldn't want to paint those!)

Within these walls are situated government buildings and the Chapel Royal of the Emerald Buddha. The buildings within the Palace are all brightly coloured and have that distinctive sloping roof design that are seen in countless movies and still photographs. Each building serves a purpose, mostly religious, and have a number of incense burners littered outside each entrance, along with shoe racks. Because the various restrictions on what we can or cannot film, it often is difficult to know what we have captured, but in these situations you simply sit back and watch the scenery.

The main attraction, The Emerald Buddha, stands (or sits) about 1.5 metres tall and is made of one-piece jade. It is an object of national veneration and crowds come to pay their respect, to the memory of Buddha, and his high teachings on certain days of the week when it is open to the public. It sits high on the gold-trimmed altar – designed to represent the traditional aerial chariot.

Kris has informed us that it is highly disrespectful to point your feet (considered to be the lowest and lesser body part) in the direction of the Buddha statue. Therefore, when sitting in admiration, you must either cross your legs or swing them around to point behind.

'The foot is the bad part of every human,' Kris explains.

I chuckle. 'Yep. One whiff of mine and you're a dead man.'

One thing I have noticed is how the Thai people follow their religious dictations diligently. Throughout the morning we have passed numerous Buddha statues or temples and, without fail, Kris and Pop acknowledge each and every one of them with a slight dip of the head and an arm movement similar to 'the sign of the cross'.

A temple of Thailand.

Our next destination for the morning is the magnificent Wat Po, home of the famous reclining Buddha – a huge gold statue lying on its side. Throughout the country there are plenty of different versions and scales of the Buddha, available as souvenirs or religious ornaments, but this one at Wat Po is clearly the biggest we have seen yet. It measures 10 metres high and 50 long, and really is a marvel in itself. While we all gasp in awe, I notice a tinny, rattling sound that echoes continuously in the giant chamber. At first I think it is water leaking or falling onto the statue, but Belinda correctly points out the chamber 'wish pots' – a cluster of metallic bowls surrounding the far perimeter of the chamber wall. Kris explains that coins are purchased and deposited, one in each pot, to represent the various wishes.

'Can we do this?' I ask Mark.

'And your three wishes, Eynon?'

'I can't tell you that.'

'Go on.'

'Three words: Rugby, World and Cup.'

Our next stop is a well kept secret and a quiet, peaceful oasis in the middle of the city, Wot Raja Bopit – a similar temple of worship. The building is situated 20 minutes south of the Grand Palace and has exactly the same architectural features. But just as we are settling into a reflective mood, the doors of a nearby school erupt into a flowing mass of children, who surround the temple in their small groups and proceed to have a 'morning break', consisting largely of games of badminton and soccer. It makes quite a bizarre sight: an ancient worshipping shrine playing host to teenage footballers. Kris assures us that this is common practice and the children are respectful.

We are now shading ourselves from the sun at every opportunity as the temperature soars to 34°C, and from the sound that our stomachs are making (plus the bedraggled look of the crew) it is suggested that a lunch break would be the best option. Mark leads us to the Wong-Nah restaurant which lies on the eastern bank of the Chao Phraya River, and immediately makes the order with Kris. This includes chicken and bamboo soup, deep fried squid, chicken and cashew mix, sweet'n'sour pork and . . . er . . . my selection . . . a cheese burger.

Much to our surprise, and obvious desire, the meal is paid for by the Thai Tourist Board so we heartily dig in. Most people are unaware of the necessity of a healthy film crew, no cameraman means no pictures . . . so we are all aware of the dangers of experimenting with exotic food. On this occasion, Belinda was orchestrating my introduction to Thai food. Within the space of an hour I had tried, tested and enjoyed every dish on the table and, like my co-workers, could only muster up the energy to stick my thumb up in the air as a sign of my appreciation – so full were our stomachs.

Mark then capped off a productive morning by announcing that we would have an unproductive afternoon – a few hours off.

Later that night, we make our way to the Raja Damneon Stadium, only down the road from the hotel, and by the sight of the thousands of spectators swarming into the arena, we know we are onto an evening of premium entertainment – Thai Boxing.

'It's a game of skill, strength and discipline. And that's if you're a spectator.'

We've been warned that filming the crowd could be dangerous as many of the gamblers, afraid of being recognised, will throw objects at the lens. This doesn't worry Ors in the slightest, and he threatens to give any perpetrators a good old Canterbury shoe-ing. One of the officials on duty is only too pleased to help us with any rule interpretation:

'So what are the restrictions when they fight?'

'There are no rules,' he chuckles, 'except for no headbutting. That was banned a few years ago.'

We enter what appears to be a scene straight out of any modern martial arts movie. The ring is brightly lit and the seating disappears into the hazy upper regions of the complex. We are not the only camera crew here and it seems that much attention is being paid to the main event of the night where the national champion (due to the different categories, there are many!) goes by the name of Tamtimdam Dremaomyai.

The entertainment begins at 7.00pm and the barrage of gamblers, touts, trainers, security guards and a military presence file into their positions. A capacity crowd is expected but there are several empty spaces. Nevertheless, the atmosphere is really heating up. The national anthem plays and the action gets under way with the first event involving two 100 pound boxers who contest the fight over 5 rounds. Quite by chance we find that a mention of New Zealander Ray Sefo seems to register a hoot of recognition from most Thai officials. Pop firmly reminds us that Sefo was world champion in one of many different categories.

Belinda gets the impression that the whole thing is rather barbaric, especially when the fight progresses into the final few rounds. The crowd noise reaches fever pitch, and there is much excitement when a fighter is knocked down. For the record, Wichit Sakmuangklang and Seankeng Thantawan are the first two fighters who entertain us, but as the night draws to a climax, the bouts get more ferocious (as the boxers get heavier) including the main event which sees world champion Tamtimdam

Dremaomyai make short work of his luckless opponent. A great night out.

6.00am: I make the gym but struggle to enthuse. Have an interesting and thoughtful conversation with a sweaty Japanese businessman who is here on this fifth visit to the city in the space of a month. He is suitably unimpressed by the climate.

'They say the heat here is like God – it's everywhere.'

Our first mission for the morning is the Bangkok Flower markets, just a five minute drive from the Grand China Princess. It consists of a large collection of bamboo and wooden stalls selling largely B-grade flowers – like New Zealand most A-grade produce is exported -in the form of daffodils, lilies and roses. The flowers are arranged in various forms, some in a crucifix, others in garden bunches or in ringed circles. Though beautiful, they aren't tempting, and once the shots are taken we wait quietly in the morning sun as Dodge and Ors venture out to take film of the traffic.

The pause in the shooting gives me an opportunity to talk to Kris about a number of issues that have arisen since we flew into the country. He is a bubbly character who has kept us well informed and satisfied throughout our brief time here. I probe him about the youth in his country – their ideals, their problems. It seems that they experience an incredibly disciplined upbringing. The family unit is highly treasured and each family member must contribute towards its overall function and cohesion. This means that many children are sent out to work as early as five years of age – and much has been made of Thailand's notoriously young prostitution industry, although Kris insists that this is restricted largely to the country areas.

Our conversation delves deeper into the subject of marriage and divorce – the latter of which is rare. The shame bought upon an individual should a relationship fail is high, and intolerable in this society. Marriage is usually only permitted by the girl's parents and will result after a long period of courtship. In Thailand, a single mother is viewed as the ultimate disgrace – girls often sent away to relatives in the countryside to avoid family ridicule and suffering.

Mark has suddenly felt the urge to do some serious shopping, so our driver escorts us into the Khet Dusit area of Bangkok. Lying east on Praram 5 Road is the world famous Central Gems International company, one of the best and biggest jewellery showrooms in Thailand and in Asia. The brochure says:

'A visit to Thailand is incomplete without a purchase of jewellery . . . your money is always worth more here'.

Very well, I think to myself, but my wallet is in the safest possible place – back at the hotel. The welcome is warm and elaborate, several traditionally dressed urchins prance and slide their way through a simple dance routine, before unloading a fruit cocktail onto all visitors. Although impressive, it's true function is to persuade customers to buy aplenty. No harm in being spoilt.

Getting past the main entrance, you then proceed past a line of work stalls displaying the various processes that are performed on each stone. From cutting to buffing, cleaning and polishing, it's all there to see as you make the final transition from the preparation to the display room. Each work station is manned by a handful of tireless workers, crouched on their tiny seats, hands dirty from work.

Some of the craftsmanship is indeed staggering, but Dodgy, our producer, points out that some of the prices seem to be higher than the New Zealand equivalent. With this in mind, everybody becomes wary of their interests. Twenty minutes later, no purchases are made despite constant coaxing from the staff, and a rather dejected host, Ratuping, waves us farewell.

Lunch, yet again, on the banks of the River Chao Phraya, which prepares us for the longtail boat ride down the Klong canals. Belinda and I are given our own vessel, which takes the form of a thin, long canoe-shaped boat with a V-8 motor attached to the back. The vehicle looks thin and flimsy but no sooner have we left the shore, we are almost airborne with such ferocity that the seating almost gives underneath. As we skim across the congested harbour the driver lets out a devilish chuckle – to the point where I am now quite concerned. My doubts are not founded as he skilfully guides us between numerous barges and vessels from the vast harbour expanse to the tricky canals that still remain Bangkok's best kept secret.

The canals stretch across the whole city, connecting some of the inner banks to the main land mass. There is a whole community operating on the water – a sight most foreigners would miss if they didn't have the luxury of travelling on the River. There is no real surprise when we discover that the city is considered to be the 'Venice of the East', and some water-based businesses (such as trading and food) are profitable industries throughout the area.

Dodgy, Jim and Ors take the other boat to capture the moments, while Belinda and I settle back in the late afternoon sun (which is very pleasant at this time) and talk. The water is not clean but is populated by numerous species of marine life, in particular catfish that are regularly fed by tourists. Our stomachs are rumbling, but food is never far away in the form of the water merchants that litter the riverside. A friendly tradesman and his wife, dressed in what looks like an old sack, casually paddle over and offer a choice of dates, bananas and coke. I settle for a bunch of bananas, which cost around NZ$1.

I wake the next morning before sunrise but feel remarkably fresh. The air-conditioning unit rumbles all night and leaves you with clogged sinuses but the noise seems to resemble torrential rain on the roof, which sends me to sleep quickly. The early wake-up is necessary if we are to catch the action down in Bangkok's central Lumphini Park. It is a gathering place for hundreds of thousands of Thais who congregate to pray, exercise, eat or simply chat with friends.

Moving around the perimeter, we pass countless groups of walkers and joggers, while the choice of ballroom dancing, tai-chi, roller blading, group prayer or aerobics seems to entertain a large number of young and old. Belinda and I join in an outdoor weightlifting session and, coincidentally, bump into the Thailand Bodybuilding Champion – he challenges me for a 'pose-down'. I lose.

The national anthem is supposed to play every morning at 8.00am, and we prepare to shoot the occasion – expecting most people to stand in respect of the tune:

'What's the time?' asks Mark.

'Almost 8.00am.' I reply.

'When it plays, I want you to talk about the significance of the tune.'

'No problem.'

I answer as the sound system crackles into life.

'Like a Rhinestone cowboy . . . .'

Hysterics all round. The DJ had mixed tapes. Clearly a Glen Campbell fan.

The van eats up the motorway as we head towards the coast for our first excursion out of the city. We stop at a petrol station for a breakfast of donuts and chippies, and Jim spots a number of salt farms nearby which glow brightly in the morning sun. Workers are scraping the top skin off the salt flats while their helpers gather the excess material and store it under massive polythene sheets. It is then left out in the sun to dry and dehydrate to create the ultimate end product – salt. In various guises, this ritual – the making of salt – has taken place since the dawn of civilisation.

Belinda Todd discovers the origin of table salt.

Three temples are visited this morning, all uniquely different. The first is Phetchaburi, a summer palace and temple that was built by Rama IV – the monarch portrayed in the film *The King and I* (which, subsequently, is still banned in Thailand because of the 'disrespect and inaccuracies'). The second is Boon Thabee Temple, which houses a number of orange-cloaked monks in its adjoining monastery. I have the honour of speaking with the Abbot, using Kris as an interpreter, about life as a monk. He explains the strict and monotonous lifestyle, but also reminds us that it is a choice to devote your life to the faith, and he accepts anything that comes with it. The third temple is Khao Banda-it, an amazing limestone cavern full of Buddhas – a real secret place visited by only Thai tourists – that is 'guarded' by swarms of wild monkeys. There is an overwhelming sense of peace and tranquillity as we descend into the cavern's depths. Apart from the familiar 'whirl' of the camera rolling, there is complete silence from all visitors for about 10 minutes. Mark breaks the calm by telling us it's time to go.

We reach the Hua Hin lookout at around 2.00pm, but the sun is still powerful on our faces. The lookout gives Steve a superb view of the breaking waves down on the Hua Hin beach, while I play with a group of playful elephants in the car park. The camp of elephant handlers (mahouts) introduce the animals, and insist on giving us a ride. Within minutes, Belinda and I are sitting on Botang, while Steve and Jim are

Camera crew catch an elephant to
their next assignment.

Belinda feeds Bo.

mounted upon Yipyip. The two babies, Yo and Bo (6 months old), stay behind with Mark. The elephants are of the Indian variety who have smaller ears, shorter bodies but higher intelligence than their African counterpart.

After the bumpy ride, we lunch at the San Thai restaurant while a group of teenage girls swim below the pier – fully clothed. We decide not to join them.

The final stop today is at the Royal Hua Hin Golf course, where Tiger Woods is due to visit and play in a few weeks. With that kind of inspiration I tee off on the famous, and wildly scenic, 14th hole. I have three attempts at getting the ball near the hole:

First ball: Shoot off directly to the right and crashed into a tree
Second ball: Rocketed to the left, staying a metre off the ground
Third ball: Perfect. Landed a metre from the hole in a complete fluke
               shot.

When we finally get back to Grand China, I sleep and dream of beating Tiger.

Another early call but some general excitement as we are travelling to the ancient Thailand capital of Ayutthaya. It was sacked and burned by the Burmese in 1767 but still retains its classic beauty. The trip takes 2 hours and by 10.00am we are all taking photographs of the stone monuments that appear around every corner. The classical Asia architecture would have been stunning in its heyday, but is still quite a sight today.

The motion picture business has been kind to Ayutthaya, with Bon Jovi shooting a music video in the ruins of various temples while the Wat Si Samphet ruin is currently being used to shoot the new *Mortal Combat II* movie. It is reported that Bon Jovi paid US$1 million as a location fee so the *Mortal Combat II* producers would be forking out some big bucks for this. We get the opportunity to talk to the crew and also the lead actor, James Reimar, who is on his third visit to Thailand. He has mastered the language and loves the way of life, especially their respect for their religion. The structured, but simple lifestyle was an inspiration to him.

The camera crew show off their moves on the set of MORTAL COMBAT II.

Considering we are on the set of a major Hollywood blockbuster, the crew are fantastic and let us wander around among the lights and cameras. The producers have recently run into trouble with local preservation groups protesting that the film company is not conserving the delicate temple structure. One publicity officer is quick to point out how the use of polystyrene props and structures prevent any damage to the surrounding walls. We return the crew's accommodating attitude by getting some footage of the 'fake' set and backdrop to prove their argument.

Another huge reclining Buddha lies resplendent in the background, this time covered with a huge orange sheet. It looks like the Buddha is undergoing construction work but Kris explains that every season heralds a new colour for the Buddha to be covered with – a sign of respect.

Due to the heavy schedule of travelling, Mark has promised a ride on the Oriental Princess cruise vessel which takes us back to Bangkok. The trip takes four hours, but is broken up by a buffet lunch and an opportunity to snooze in the afternoon sun on the deck. A gentle breeze keeps the temperature down, and we all recline in the white deck-chairs. Four hours goes very quickly.

A late night out at a local Thai restaurant means none of the crew emerge from their rooms until well after lunchtime. A quick look around the Yao Waraj market place to buy a few travel accessories – batteries, drink and a book for our plane trip tomorrow morning.

Dodge and Steve travel out Ma Boon Krong and the World Trade Center for more shopping and we all meet up at the Dance Fever disco nightclub in the centre of town. We are greeted by a security force dressed in bright blue overalls who park the car, another crew of red-coated gentlemen usher you in while girls in green dresses serve you drinks. The nightclub is situated in a large warehouse, with the walls covered in television screens and a concert stage at the far end. We are treated to a complete mix of dance, rock and house music while several bands, and Spice Girls impersonators, perform various numbers for the crowd.

Steve is the tallest man in the club and I rock with laughter each time he accidentally elbows some poor Thai youth in the head on the dance-floor. I manage to get up on stage to thank the people of Bangkok for their hospitality, Dodge, Mark and Jim make the most of the local brew while Pop looks on with satisfaction. It has been an amazing week of adventure and beauty for all of us – thanks largely to Mark's organisation. It will be sad to leave, as we have grown fond of Bangkok but India calls. Plenty of singing and celebrating on our way home.

Chapter 3 | India

Day 14, Sunday 26th January

I don't usually bother with writing about our travel in between destinations in my diary. The monotony of the checking-in and the flight schedule does not usually provide any wild adventure worth noting. However, you can probably anticipate the potential threat to all cohesion that flying to India could provide and, sure enough, the nightmarish scenario began as we left Bangkok International.

Another early departure to contend with. When the plane is due to depart at 8.35am, we usually allow two and a half hours to begin the laborious procedure of submitting 20 pieces of luggage to customs. This means leaving the hotel in good time, gear packed and onboard with your own personal luggage intact. A sensible wake-up call would be around 5.00am. Together with flights and check-in, this prompts a 'working' day often more tiring than one spent shooting scenery.

We leave Bangkok in economy class and arrive in Hong Kong at around midday. We bump into Anita McNaught who will accompany us to India. It also provides us with a quick chance to grab some melon and Russian broth in the VIP lounge before jumping aboard the Mumbai-bound Cathay flight at 3.00pm. The captain causes some mild panic within the 'DPE' ranks when he announces the arrival time in Bangkok.

'Bangkok?' we all scream in unison. The stewardess then assures us that we stopover in Bangkok for an hour before heading to Mumbai (Bombay). This leaves us questioning the reason behind flying to Hong Kong in the first place. We will spend 12 hours travelling to and from Bangkok.

By 5.00pm, we are back where we started. Bangkok. I humorously suggest that we call in and see Kris. Dodge gives me a hard intense look. He is not pleased. Travelling in circles is hardly good motivation when you do your best to cut corners, if you know what I mean. The arrival in

Mumbai heralded new territory for me. I had never expressed, with no disrespect, a real interest to visit India or Pakistan after hearing numerous horror stories about the Kiwi cricket teams fighting with health and hygiene.

Nevertheless I was rather captivated by the city that emerged through the cloudy evening as the plane descended. Sadly this was the only beauty any of us were to experience in Mumbai, the International Arrivals lounge proving to be a shabby collection of derelict corridors and crumbling walls. Immigration was based in a 'shed' and took an hour to process the passports. I must point out that these are observations and not criticisms – as an international traveller, you learn to become tolerant and accepting of a country's policies and procedures.

On a personal note, I had developed a rough stomach over the last couple of days due to a bad piece of chicken and was struggling with my toilet visits. Every time my tummy ached, my bowels moved – quickly.

'Dodge, I need to shit.'

'Don't be rude.'

'I'm serious mate. I'm dying here.'

'Hold onto it. We'll be in our hotel in a few hours.'

As you would expect, the pains became more intense when we arrived in Mumbai and I raced off to find the nearest toilet. I discovered the 'Men's Room' which turned out to be a couple of holes in the ground and more excrement on the walls than in the loo. You could hardly see the walls through the swarm of flies and mosquitoes, and the stench was enough to wake the dead.

I fished out a couple of pieces of paper from my pocket, and delivered. My eyes were closed through the whole procedure, and I made an effort to run fast when I had finished. I swore never to complain about the state of toilets in New Zealand ever again.

There was some respite in our rather hot and bustled adventure. The correct departure terminal was found, after wading our way through the throng of people waiting outside the Arrivals door, and the Executive Lounge provided an opportunity to sit and relax. The crew settled into a game of mini Monopoly while I lay horizontal on an old couch and watched Pete Sampras destroy his opposition in the Australian Open. Home seems so far away.

I have slipped into a restless sleep, compounded by the day's travel and a stomach full of rampant rhinos. Woke in time for our boarding call, which led to a bizarre sequence of events. In the space of 30 minutes we were given at least 5 different gate numbers, and no-one had a clue where we should be boarding our plane. We became marooned in a barren departure lounge wondering what to do. We hadn't seen a Western face or anyone who could speak English so the situation was becoming hopeless.

Things became desperate when we realised the departure time had been passed and we weren't any closer to being on the plane. My stomach was screaming for some relief, Dodge was beside himself with fear of losing 20 bags on board a flight to Delhi, while Jim just sat and shrugged his shoulders. Suddenly an airport official burst into the lounge:

'Kiwis? Kiwis? Your plane is leaving.'

'What?'

'Your plane is leaving!'

'We were told the plane would be boarding at this gate. Gate 20.'

'No, it's leaving at Gate 1.'

'Why weren't we fucking told?!'

'Gate 1. Gate 1. You must go!'

A continued chorus of shouting and debating echoed around the airport as irate security officers blamed us for being late while we retorted with the fact that no-one had told us where to go. All this resulted in a mad sprint to the other end of the terminal to find that our plane had been waiting on the tarmac for 15 minutes. We managed to stumble abroad and ventured on our 4th trip in 20 hours.

Eynon does Delhi.

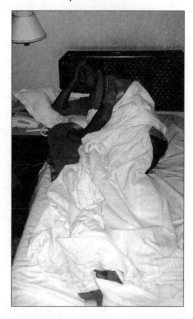

The flight to Delhi passed quickly and we were collected at the airport by the biggest mini-bus I have laid my eyes on. Everyone is subdued as we make our way to the hotel. The nightmare is almost over. It is now 6.00am in the morning but it could be midnight for all that we know. My condition has gotten worse and an immediate dosage of pills is prescribed as I fall into bed.

A knock at the door. It's Steve.

'Have some of these.'

He hands me some diarrhoea tablets.

'I don't have the runs at the moment. I'm just really tired.'

'Well, you'll want some of these then.'

He thrusts me a couple of sleeping pills.

'If these don't work, just watch the Indian movie channel. You'll be snoring in seconds.'

I am sweating profusely but it is cold. The bed sheets are soaked in a few hours, but I have the luxury of a clean, useable toilet. It is a long night.

Sporadic periods of sweaty sleep punctuate a night of toilet visits and coughing fits. Eventually the only comfort came in sitting upright in the chair beside my bed. The TV doesn't work – no real surprise – so my Walkman provides the only stimulation. The discomfort that my stomach is experiencing is not painful, just awkward. I am still unable to determine the cause – could be a number of things.

The phone rings at 8.00am. It is Dodge:

'How are ya?' he asks.

'Not bad. Just uncomfortable. I'm going to the loo every twenty.'

'Hours? That's okay then . . . .'

'Minutes. Every twenty minutes.'

'Oh.'

A quick team talk determines my fate. I am to spend the day in bed, just as a precaution. At this stage of the shoot, it is imperative that we prevent any possible illness – no replacements can be shipped in – so food must be cooked, water must be bottled and pills taken.

Not a great deal of entertainment in my bedroom. I haven't even got the energy to open my own blinds, but manage to order room service food consisting of boiled rices and potato fritters.

Meanwhile, the *Destination Planet Earth* ships sails on without me. The crew are experiencing Delhi with the New and the Old being the central theme of contrast. Old and new, rich and poor, ugly and stunningly beautiful, dirty and clean but, most of all, chaos and order. The old is Old World and Old Delhi and caste system and colour and traffic you won't believe, together with the chaos of riding a rickshaw through the streets of the old town. The new is New Delhi with the legacy of the Raj a bitter and pungent aftertaste leaving hellish bureaucratic systems in place, and the government buildings reminiscent of Washington D.C and green and khaki uniforms on every street corner.

A full night of sleep indicates a mild recovery, so I bound downstairs for an early breakfast in the hotel dining room. Steve and Jim look surprised as I dive into the plate full of sausages, but 3 days of rice and water has given me a ravenous appetite. By 9.00am, my stomach has settled and I'm raring to go!

Old Delhi discovers Anita McNaught.

We meet our Indian liaison officer, Dinesh, and our drivers. They seem like happy fellas, and are pleased I have made a speedy recovery. Three days in bed has numbed my senses slightly, as the noise and atmosphere in the streets seems very animated and frantic. The bus winds its way through the dusty inner city to the landmark at the heart of Old Delhi, The Red Fort. The hive of activity is phenomenal as the streets quickly fill with old cattle, rickshaws, cars, bicycles and other ridiculous modes of transport all trying to get to the same place at different times – or is it the other way round?

Anita and I have the privilege of our photograph being taken by a 100 year old camera, the result looking like a couple of old pioneer settlers in a 19th century expedition. Dodge hires us a rickshaw and we proceed to ride among the backstreets past silk and sari shops, silverware stalls and food vendors. Horns toot and people shout constantly in order to negotiate the traffic madness but everyone seems to find a way through. Eventually our driver, who assures me he is adequately qualified, crashes several times. Despite the trail of destruction, it all adds to the excitement.

We arrive at the Delhi Mosque and wade our way through a sea of beggar children to get to the front door. Most of them are blackened from sleeping in the filthy gutters, and most are missing limbs – one 8 year-old girl has no legs and carries a 10 month old child. It is disturbing to see but you have to refuse their pleas or they won't leave you alone.

The Mosque provides a moment of peace in the middle of this madness, despite the refusal of the guards to let the camera gear into the main prayer courtyard. Steve smuggles in the 'digital video camera' to do the job.

A new member of the party, Aruna (a local aristocrat) suggests a nearby market place in which to view a traditional dancing display. It's only around the corner from the hotel, and we are greeted by an array of classical and cultural stick dancing. We are encouraged to participate, and I am invited to join in with the band. Drumming and dancing entertains Steve and I, while Jim and Dodge muse over a selection of saris and coloured blankets.

Our road trip begins the following morning.

Agra is our destination and we are on the road by 8.00am. Guri is our driver, and he entertains us with numerous stories of life on the highway. There is only one road between Agra and Delhi and it is in bad need of repair. Potholes and aging asphalt create a bumpy and unpleasant journey.

The highway is notoriously dangerous at night, due to stray cattle and armies of bandits, so the majority of shooting will occur during daylight hours to prevent any night-time travel. On the journey, we encounter a whole array of cattle and cars.

Occasionally a lone bicycle rider will pedal his way into Guri's path, but no matter what mode of transport is being used it is guaranteed that the horn will be in perfect working order. The horn plays a different role in India than New Zealand, used unaggressively to warn trucks and carts that you are within their vicinity.

I take a few minutes to observe Guri's 'horn' antics and discover that he uses it an average 20 times a minute.

'How can you do this trip so often?' I ask.

'I have no choice my friend. It is the only way.'

'Not too many accidents I suppose.'

'Plenty. But mostly cows. They are a motorist's nightmare.'

A halfway stop at the 'Castle Inn' provides a lunch of cheese omelette and French toast. Guri shows us how to bowl off spin in the car park. Steve shows us how to play an off drive, while I show them all how to streak.

After 6 hours on the road, we finally arrive at the Taj Mahal – the monument to 'love' that took 20,000 people 22 years to build. The King constructed the Taj Mahal in memory of his daughter but was then banished to the Agra Fort – where he was confined to a solitary room. Kuldeep is the official Tourist representative who has had the honour of guiding the Clinton family and numerous Australian cricket teams around the vast grounds of the Taj.

If British Rail think they have problems, then it is some surprise that the Indian Railway company even functions. The Agra Fort Railway Station is busy, and stinks of urine. The locals swarm around the camera, which makes filming rather difficult, but we persevere and are rewarded with some stunning images. No Indian experience seems to be complete without a train ride on the second largest rail system in the world.

One is a legend. The other is the Taj Mahal.

At any one time there are up to 700 trains operating around the country. The railway has always played an important part in unifying the various outposts of this massive territory.

Dodge encounters familiar problems of obtaining filming permission on the platform from the station officials, but ever-vigilant Steve continues to roll. I talk to several young men whose eyes light up at the mention of a certain sporting icon:

'Yes, we're from New Zealand,' I answer their query.

'Ah, the home of Richerrid Headry,' they exclaim with much enthusiasm.

'Richerrid Headry – world famous, world famous,' shouts another.

Richard Hadlee has never been better exalted.

The idea of punctuality doesn't seem to exist as a rusty series of carriages pull into the platform. Four hours late. Our train is only three minutes late which is some small consolation in the midst of this stinking, sweaty mess. We climb aboard 2nd Class and Anita comments: 'Next stop, Auschwitz!' which seems to accurately describe the train experience.

Anita and Peta Carey brave the Indian rail system.

The train slugs away from the platform a half hour from the correct departure time but we have been enlightened and entertained by the throng of commuters gathered in our carriage. The interior consists of nothing more than a few decrepit wooden blocks as seats and iron bars attached, some by string, to the wooden frame.

If India is a nation where a bus crash can kill 150 people, work out what a deathtrap the trains are!

Our destination is Fatehpur Sikri, a trip that takes one and a half hours through the arid countryside littered with broken sewer pipes, muddied rivers, remote villages and poverty aplenty. Despite a number of beggars on the trackside, there is no obvious evidence that depression affects these people. They have plenty to complain about but, even in the heat of adverse conditions, the women remain impeccably groomed and the men always smiling.

The train trip ends and we disembark to be collected by Guri and the van at Fatehpur and to begin the drive to Panch Mahal – a scenic fort with a wealth of surrounding landscape. We climb the four sets of stairs for the ultimate view.

'All this climbing has given me an appetite!' says Peta. We all agree heartily and our hunger pangs led us to Penpasar for a mighty meal of rice and chicken. More physical exercise in the form of bike riding in the Keoladeo Bird Sanctuary. The opportunity to spot kingfisher, storks and cranes, while Steve and Jim are pedalled in a rickshaw. One circuit of the Park is adequate, Guri is starting to get concerned over the setting sun – it will soon be too dark to drive. The road to Jaipur is long and winding. And bumpy.

I've woken up in a different city, again. Jaipur is the old capital city that once held a population of 160,000 within its terracotta walls. It is now the home to two and a half million Indians.

Another temple on the schedule this morning. A great view of Jaipur from the elevated Sun Monument as Anita wanders down the orange

DESTINATION ANYWHERE

The Sun Temple, Agra.

corridors inside while I pose for photographs on the towering stone steps. A number of goats, cows and cats loiter aimlessly at the base of the temple. Our excursion leads us into the heart of the Pink City – as it is known by the locals – gathering its name from the surrounding stone wall which zigzags its way through the thriving metropolis. It divides the old from the new; the ancient relics of the past contrasted with the stunning design of modern architecture.

Peta insists on stopping for a lassi – a local drink made up of yoghurt and cream – at the Lassi Walla. The drink is served in terracotta cups which can be disposed of once you've consumed the product. A quick scull is followed by a chorus of terracotta demolition in the nearby rubbish bin. The drink is given the 'thumbs up' by the whole crew.

Tradition goes down the plughole when we order lunch from the Moten Badi restaurant:

'We'll have five rounds of japati and chicken and one pizza.'

'Sorry, sir?'

'Pizza. For the boy.' Dodge points my way.

I just shrug my shoulders and explain that I have been ill.

Our Delhi guide, Dinesh, has been replaced by the Rajistan

Come in Sinbad, your time is up:
Eynon does elephant.

We're beginning to get used to this
novel mode of transport.

representative, Sharm, who is given a warm welcome by the crew. He immediately leads us to the Jai Observatory and explains how astrology plays a significant role in the lives of the population. Most Indians have their maiden names determined by the day on which they were born, and whom they marry is directly related to the month in which you are conceived. Sharm also displays a hidden talent for palm reading, so I forcefully thrust my meaty digits in front of him:

'Ah, you have fine hands Nick. You will live a long life,' he predicts.

Hmm, that's a bit too general for my liking so I ask him about marriage.

'By looking at your romance line, I can see two marriages in your lifetime (God forbid!) and your wife will give birth to three children. You will also be very wealthy too.'

I must look over my contract when I get back to New Zealand.

'But you will have heart trouble when you reach the age of sixty.'

This last statement rapidly transforms my elation to concern. However, Sharm assures me that I will find good health in my later years. His warmth and sincerity cloud any doubt, and I find him very convincing. Jim and Steve rush into line to get a quick glimpse of their future. Unlike most palm-readers, he doesn't charge a bean.

The day finishes observing a massive prayer ceremony at the Farewell Temple in the centre of Jaipur. The session proves to be a hugely spiritual event with hundreds of church-goers chanting and singing in unison around a brightly decorated altar. All I see is Steve's head, with camera, bobbing between the praying masses.

Our last day in India is used to shoot pick-ups of the Amber Fort and the Rambagh Palace before we travel back to Delhi. The week has been long and tiring, but surprisingly rewarding as we sit back in the comfort of our air-conditioned bus. The heavy strains of Paul Weller play on the stereo, and Guri is furiously tooting his way through the traffic. We have witnessed poverty at its most extreme in India, people who have clutched on to the 'bottom rung' of life for so long, people who have stared into the face of adversity since their birth, but one thing is glaringly obvious about the native residents of India: They always have a smile on their faces, and seem to accept the hand they have been dealt.

Although I have found the country to be incredibly intense and it requires a patient effort to get anything done, it has been thoroughly rewarding. An experience we shall never forget.

Still, was there a sight more welcoming than the tarmac of Auckland airport when we arrived? I think not.

CHAPTER 4 | # FRANCE

Day 22, Saturday 22nd February

We encounter problems before the plane leaves the airport. Our soundman Jim Henderson has not been issued a work visa for France, and will have to travel to Wellington to get it sorted before he even begin his long haul to Paris. New Zealanders are exempt from certain immigration laws but Jim, being Australian, will now have to catch a later plane. It's not a disaster, just an unfortunate disruption.

We arrive in Hong Kong to find that our connecting flight will have to be delayed until the morning due to engine trouble so the spooky 'omens' continue to plague our shoot – before we've even started! The airport officials transport a number of very irate passengers to the Regent Riverside Hotel for a couple of hours sleep.

Before we know it, we are Paris-bound and I strike up conversation with a French girl – who is much more skilful at computer games than I am. The delays and the long flight have made things very uncomfortable for the crew. Paul Dodge (the series producer) is accompanied by Caterina De Nave (the Topp Twins director) for the shoot, and the Twins will be joining us later tomorrow.

The dusk of early evening falls over the city as we arrive at Charles de Gaulle International Airport and a combination of friendly and helpful officials plus prompt baggage service enables the crew to waltz through the exit doors within 20 minutes of arriving.

We meet Benedict and Irene (our guides for the week) who drive us through the heart of Paris to the Comfort Hotel in the central city area. The rush hour traffic and Saturday night vibes fill the streets with hundreds of vehicles and scantily dressed party-goers. The evening is chilly but refreshing.

Because of the clear weather, Dodge takes us out into the thick of the night action. In situations like this, Steve relies on the DVC camera (digital, and therefore more compact and smaller than the broadcast-size

Betacam) so we can mingle without attracting a crowd. Despite the attempt at being as inconspicuous as possible, several groups of idiot Frenchmen spoil our shots.

We wake up early and feel awful due to the disorientation and fatigue. It's the only drawback of travelling all the time and never settling into a time zone for a long time.

My room lies above the street and I spend a half an hour watching people wander the streets. The temperature is pleasant but for a slight nip in the air. It is currently spring and they are expecting another nice week of weather.

A huge day of filming ahead. First, it's off to the 15th Quarter to the market place – selling all sorts of items, fruit, huge strawberries, horse meat, English newspapers. Our French guide Benedict and I walk and talk. Food plays a big part in Parisian and French life and people seem to make such a fantastic living from eating/growing. Most of the produce is grown around the local areas and wines are also locally produced. I experiment with the local cheeses and sausages.

'Bonjour, monsieur. Parlez Anglais, um . . . just give us some cheese would ya?'

Onto the Metro which has a 'carte orange' (budget travel card) that costs NZ$20 which enables you to travel for 7 days around the Paris underground. Comparisons are often made between the London and Paris rapid-transport systems but there doesn't seem to be a huge difference. The prices are similar, they are both tidy and the trains are punctual. We travel up and down the 'Line-Rouge' before disembarking.

We climb the Arc de Triomphe – scene of a recent bombing scare – which offers great view of the Champs Elysée and surrounding areas. Although we are rushed for time, Dodge takes the opportunity to snap a couple of shots with the promotion camera. My hair is a mess this morning so I look like a complete git.

Time for a bit of culture and on to the Louvre. I make no secret of my dislike of museums and galleries, but the art on display in this particular institution is exceptional. Sadly, the place is full of stinking tourists (much like ourselves) and it is cramped and noisy. However, the works of Michelangelo leave us with gaping jaws. Dodge points me in the direction of a famous portrait:

'Nick, go and have a look at that painting'

'The one that looks like the Mona Lisa?'

'That's because it is.'

'What?'

'The Mona Lisa.'

'The Mona Lisa?'

'Yep.'

'What? You mean THE Mona Lisa?'

I am standing two metres from Leonardo Di Vinci's most famous portrait:

'She's a spunk.'

'She's a bit old for you mate – she'd be well into her hundreds now.'

Something different is provided by the Prere La Chaise graveyard, where the likes of Rosini, Chopin, Oscar Wilde and, most famously, Jim Morrison are all buried. Cameras are permitted within the boundaries of the graveyard but are banned from filming Morrison's grave. A special request from his family prevents even Polaroid shots from being taken.

In true 'DPE' style, we roll the camera and capture glimpses of his headstone.

To finish the day, we travel around the Paris walls to capture the forbidding, silhouetted figure of the Eiffel Tower. We return to the van to find Cedric waiting patiently.

Ah, Paris!

Head hit the pillow around 7.00pm and slept straight through to 6.00am – 11 hours of blissful slumber. Enough to put you back on track. I watch a report on CNN that there has been a shooting on the viewing platform of the Empire State Building – a place that we're heading next week. We have visited cities and destinations around the globe where certain events have coincided with our shoots.

A sleep-in before the Topp Twins arrive in the early morning. Jim has sorted out his visa problems so we are well on track. They are required to shoot several pieces before lunch so our group splits into two: The Twins, Caterina, Jim and Steve leave for the Central Shopping Centre while Dodge and I go museum-hunting.

For the Twins and Jim to work straight after getting off the plane is a tough call – but a necessary one. Dodge and I make our first trip to the Musée Dorsey, an impressionist museum with work from Monet, Cezanne and Van Gogh to name a few. The museum has been especially opened for us this morning and we take advantage of the empty aisles.

We meet up with Andrea Creighton – a fellow Kiwi studying opera in Paris – who is considered to be a top talent in her field. Critics have predicted future success for the diminutive prodigy, in a field that many consider to be more cut throat and ruthless than ballet or modelling. In a typically small world, I discover she was educated down the road from my home in Wellington. We spend a few hours catching up with local news: (this type of conversation is very common with most New Zealanders).

'Do you know Charlotte Cummings?'

'Yep, I went to school with her brother.'

'He played rugby for Marist, didn't he?'

'Yep, and his mum coached my sister in netball.'

'He's in London now with Jim Thorpe.'

'Oh, really?'

She has grasped the French language and is able to offer plenty of good advice and information about the city. She has free time near the end of the week, and has agreed to show us around some nightspots. Her most valuable tip: 'walk to find the really secret spots!' A tip worth noting.

As far as European cities go, she thinks that Paris is more spread out and diverse. Parisians aren't too outward, you need to get amongst them to get the real feeling for France.

Break for lunch. Café du Commerce. Irene and Benedict have reserved two large tables. Everyone orders the specialty from the waiter – salmon. I order the steak, but keep well clear of the snails. The rain starts to pour outside, and Jim almost faints with the fatigue of jetlag.

Pop into the Musée de Picasso. A popular choice for the local school children as the place is packed. Some as young as 5 years – I wonder if these French youngsters appreciate this massive cultural asset? Paintings, sculptures and artefacts from a man who was clearly obsessed and passionate about his artwork. A tortured genius.

Our final call today is M. Poulain's Bread Shop. He is well known all over the world for his breadmaking skills. He sells mostly in the US and Western Europe but distributes worldwide. Quite an animated character, who is a good friend of Salvador Dali – has made edible furniture for him. 'Bread chandeliers', bread bed and a wholemeal sofa adorn the display room. The smell, the touch, the feeling of the bread makes it different in so many ways:

'You must tell New Zealand to come to see my bread. I will welcome them with open arms and a taste of my wares,' he splutters in broken English, 'I will sell them my beautiful bread furniture.'

I have an image of turning up to Immigration with a giant bread sofa. NZ Customs would have a field day. Monsieur Poulain offers us cream tarts and coffee, and I get a photo taken with the bread chandelier.

Jim is starting to suffer from severe lack of sleep. There is a Burger King across the road, so I do the burger run for the team. The hotel rooms are tiny, so we are unable to set up the equipment to watch the day's rushes (the recorded tapes). Everybody votes for any early bed anyway. By 11.00pm, the corridors of the Comfort Hotel are silent, except for the occasional snore coming from Room 615: Jim Henderson.

Busy traffic sounds outside my window in the early hours but another sound sleep. Printemps Shopping Arcade is hosting a new season fashion show and we have all been lucky enough to be invited. The show is top-class with some equally impressive talent wearing the items. The models are all several notches off the top level, but are still full-time professionals. Winter wear from Yves St. Laurent seems to be the popular item. Afterwards, I talk to the show co-ordinator and she explains the importance of fashion to Parisians.

'What you wear determines what you are. Your personality determines what clothes you are most comfortable with.'

DESTINATION ANYWHERE

I have a wardrobe of tracksuit pants and sweatshirts. I must be lacking in something. Being young, dumb and impressed by the talent on show today, I inquire about the often-controversial world of modelling and try to dispel some of the unfavourable myths attached:

'The models used for our shows are not under as much pressure as the super and mega model personalities. Our models are more cosmopolitan, several have children and none of them struggle with any eating disorders. The majority of our roster come from Africa, Sweden and Corsica but are part of a select few. The competitive nature of being a model is extreme. Most are burnt out by the age of 30.'

'Could I ever consider a career in modelling?' I ask with an ounce of ambition.

'No,' she replies bluntly. 'You are too short'

Lunch at Littlejoys before we cruise the river in a glass bottom boat. A windy and wet affair though a fantastic chance to see the sights from a different prospective. Two pleasant crew members provide the commentary. They are both students and this is a tourism course appointment. Good experience but a crap job – even though they enjoy the opportunity to test their English and PE skills. Back to the hotel for a quick rest and then onto the Mondon rugby club (south of Paris) to train and play against the local corporate side.

It has to be the coldest night of the year and the mud has already caked my body. I am playing halfback for the home side, and have been getting soundly destroyed around the base of the scrum. They like to play the game at pace and love to run the ball from all corners. Dirty play peppers the game and I become a little hesitant to get fully involved in any fights due to some frightful 'haymakers' being thrown by the monstrous opposition front row.

I play the second half and get bathed in ruck marks and cuts – difference between dirty and rough play. All of a sudden, I feel very inadequate. My team finishes strongly and eventually wins the game. In a somewhat bizarre twist, the referee's whistle is blown and each player proceeds to kiss and cuddle his opposite number. I feint a pulled hamstring and hobble off to the sideline.

The lads in the changing room are pleased with the result – quite an achievement to play and survive in France. Back to the Comfort Inn for an ice pack and a warm bath.

Avec les TOPP TWINS.

The aches and pains of last night's rugby become a little more pronounced. Early wake to film travel tips (Big city be careful, exchange rate will give you 4 francs to NZ$1. Restaurants cost twice as much as brasseries – will serve you food all day)

On to St. Michael's Church and marketplace to shoot faces and places. Linda and Jools, dressed as Camp Mother and Camp Leader get the chance to have portraits painted. The French don't quite know what to think of the Camps – they look on in amazement.

To the Paris Opera House to listen to our friend Andrea sing in front of a packed house. Impressive acoustics and an active crowd who enjoy the free performance of the Academy's developing talent. Andrea's Irish friend Sam joins us to say hello and introduce himself. He is a good friend of Andrea's and together they are forging a path towards ultimate opera success.

The evening activities include a visit to the Moulin Rouge for a topless dancing display. A juggler, a contortionist and a dog performer are highlights but the star happens to be an Australian dancer called Maurice. We pounce into her dressing room as she is getting prepared and talk to her about her life and profession. Getting your boobs out on stage can't be easy, but she is a seasoned veteran and performs with a high level of professionalism. Her current title is a result of years of training and discipline. As she says: 'Hundreds of slammed doors, but one opened for me.'

Following the interview, we sit and watch the hour-long performance. We discover that the Moulin Rouge show is a little more than just topless dancing – it is a carefully choreographed dance display by a cast of several hundred performers. Plus boobs.

Food and drink is provided, and the team gets a chance to enjoy each other's company for the first time this week – all nine of us squashed into a corner table for two.

Jim and I are beginning to enjoy Burger King so we make a late night call for fries and a Whopper Burger. I'm growing fat. But I don't care.

The Twins travel to Yves St. Laurent the next morning to get a facial. Plenty of thrills for them both. Dodge and I check out Lanvin – the top suit shop in Paris. They specialise in custom made suits, trousers and hats (for the Roland Garosse Tennis Tournament) Spoke to Mr Javert about the suits, trousers and tailoring – hugely expensive, out of my league. Such is their popularity that clients fly in from as far away as Iraq and Saudi Arabia. Your average sports sweatshirt costs around NZ$700. I explain to Mr Javert that I am only looking – not buying. He expresses his disappointment by buying us a coffee.

The afternoon is free so we meet up with Sam and Andrea at Café Bastille for a quiet dinner and then to Sans Sans – a trendy bar and nightclub with heavy bass sounds – House of Pain, Onyx, Naughty by Nature. A great chance for the crew to kick back and relax. Free drinks and free T-shirts given away by the friendly bouncers. At the conclusion of the evening we all go our separate ways. Andrea is living 20 minutes away, so we drop her off.

Final shooting day begins with a nice, relaxing walk through the streets. We travel to the Eiffel Tower to capture the rising sun. Always very important in a show, but we don't have the luxury of several takes to get it right. The sun is bright and warm today. We have been incredibly lucky with the weather – not only this week but also prior to Christmas. Every European destination has been in the throes of either deep winter or early spring – we expected lousy weather but it has been excellent.

Nôtre Dame Cathedral is our final visit and the view in the afternoon sun is amazing. They are halfway through cleaning the exterior (happens every few years) due to pollution and I'm not sure if I like it this way. Almost too clean. When it comes to ancient architecture, old is good.

The inside is impressive, though too dark to shoot. Despite the swarming mass of tourists we're told it's not a popular day to visit. God forbid what it would be like in the summer.

The Centre Stone of Paris is situated here (all roads in France lead towards this point) so strict filming restrictions apply but, yet again, that does not prove to be an obstacle. We could get away with murder and not be arrested in this city. The final shot is made – The Topp Twins and myself wandering off into the distance – before Steve dissembles the tripod and packs the case away, and declares the shoot to be complete.

CHAPTER 5 | # NEW YORK

Day 29, Saturday 1ˢᵗ March

European breakfasts are beginning to win me over. The choice of rolls and filling make a pleasant change from greasy bacon and eggs. Steve carries a mountain of food on his plate in anticipation of the long day ahead. We have received a fax this morning that completely outlined our travel arrangements from here to Cape Town. Due to costs and seat availability, the airline cannot possibly fly transatlantic to New York which would take all of 7 hours. Instead, the route will take us to Hong Kong onto Vancouver and then New York – a complete circumnavigation of the world (ie: from Auckland to Hamilton via Invercargill) While this news isn't thrilling, we accept it as written word and get on with packing our luggage into Cedric's van.

Rugby union news has also drifted into the general communication, as the first Super 12 results filter through. Auckland drawing with Northern Transvaal and ACT winning over Queensland. The French newspapers carry headlines of the France v England clash that takes place later this afternoon. These snippets of news provide a light moment within the crew.

Charles de Gaulle Airport is choking with the huge number of passengers, and we take almost an hour to check-in the luggage. Sad farewells to Benedict, Irene and Cedric followed by a slow amble to the 'back of the bus'. Due to heavy booking, we have been issued Economy seats and accept our sentence with glum faces. Being small of frame and short of leg the seats in Economy are reasonably comfortable for my stature, but Steve (at nearly 6 foot 4 inches) really struggles.

This cramped posture is maintained for a nightmarish 10 hours before we 'stride' into the spacious Business Lounge of Hong Kong Airport. A further wait of 5 hours before we board another bound for Vancouver. Imovane pills are consumed for purpose of promoting sleep but we can only doze lightly.

The night blends into day and, before we know it, the distant hills of Vancouver stare at us through morning fog as we touch down. The groggy haze of jetlag has set in and I feel like I have been awake for several days as we gather in the transit lounge. Jim looks ten years older and Steve has given up talking, while I run my walkman batteries dry.

An hour turns into two before the boarding call is made. Everything seems to be turning to shit – in a manner of speaking. The toilets in the lounge have flooded, they've run out of food and the announcement microphone has broken. One big bloody nightmare.

'What day is it?' Jim asks.

'I don't care,' mumbles Steve.

'I don't know,' is my only answer.

Our marathon journey enters its final stage and the five hour flight (in economy again!) goes quickly. I don't have the enthusiasm to eat or watch movies. With hair and body smelling old and musky, we stumble into the Arrivals Lounge of JFK International Airport. We clamber into the welcoming arms of Nigel Carpenter – this week's director – who immediately notices the strained, sleepless expressions on our faces.

He greets us, helps to pack the bags and orders immediate sleep in the comfort of the Pennsylvania Hotel – which stands directly opposite Madison Square Gardens in the city centre.

My head hits the pillow after a quick shower and I contemplate the events of the last three days. I never want to do that kind of journey again. Travelling almost entirely around the world in 80 hours has probably reduced our life expectancy considerably. The problem is I know full well that the journey to Cape Town next week will be just as tedious.

We wake up feeling awful – a bit of flu on the way. A symptom perhaps of the hectic travel schedule. New York City is alive from the first early light. Eddie turns up with the car and we head straight for the Empire State Building. 102 stories up and under heavy security presence following last week's shooting spree which resulted in the death of a young man. Same place where Meg Ryan and Tom Hanks met in the film *Sleepless in Seattle* and King Kong had a climb up the side.

It's absolutely freezing at the top so we only need one take before we are sent shivering inside. Had some time to capture action shots on the street and spoke to some of the genuine New Yorkers. Americans are always so forward and upfront and each has a story to tell. Good or bad, they will say whatever is on their minds:

'So what's it like living in New York?'

'The happiest day of my life will be when I leave this shithole!'

'It's great to work here. But to live here? No way!'

'This can be the happiest and saddest place to be in at one time.'

'Centre of the universe, man!'

Diverse opinions.

Back to the hotel to be collected by our taxi driver, Eddie, who is originally from Ghana and has been resident here for 7 years. He's a great guy, who is quite philosophical about life. He reveals that New York is a world of its own. Different races, different cultures. Is not as dangerous as one would think.

Yes, Jim, it's life as we know it: the Big Apple.

For this particular segment of the show, we were going to link up with a genuine American cabbie. Surprisingly it takes several attempts to find one that speaks English. The old image of weather-beaten, cigar-smoking locals is wrong. However, Eddie is fantastic talent and we enjoy riding around, listening to his conversation:

'Hey, y'know that people get this impression that dis place is full of bad-ass mothafuckers, man. Dat is the wrong image. You can walk da streets at 3.00am in da morning and no-one will touch ya.'

Onto 5th Avenue where Anita McNaught (this week's co-presenter) and I get kitted up for a roller blade. We try bravely to negotiate ourselves between cabs, trucks and the odd pedestrian and do several takes before Nigel, anticipating a major accident, ushers us off the road. It was good fun. With skating on the mind, we head down into Central Park to the natural ice rink. We swap 'rollers' for 'blades' and proceed to crash, wallop and bang into each other. The snow is beginning to fall gently onto the ice and conjures up images of a 'White Christmas in New York' feeling. Or perhaps *Gorky Park*.

FAO Schwartz is the one of the biggest toy stores in the world, so big

Skating on thin ice, Central Park.

in fact that Michael Jackson shops here. When he does, they close the whole place off for him. An incredible amount of variety, packed into three floors. Oscar the Grouch, Star Wars, Barbie and Cabbage Patch kids in abundance – a youngster's dream. There is a scene from the motion picture *Big* when Tom Hanks plays an oversized piano with his feet – it was filmed here at FAO Schwartz and the moment is relived when I attempt my version of 'tickling the ivories' with my toes.

'I never knew you could get so many different Barbie dolls,' says Jim.

'Especially a lifesize version,' I point out. No further comment.

The next morning it's down to the Metro – which is far more confusing than London's Tube on this bitterly cold morning. We made our way from 34th Street to South Ferry station to catch the Staten Island Ferry. Only 50 cents return – what value! The trip took 30 minutes and gave us the chance to film the Manhattan skyline in great detail. The weather is dull, grey and not ideal for shooting but it's nice to get some fresh air. The Sports Illustrated Swimsuit Edition has just been released so there is a frantic search of nearly every newsstand to find a copy:

'*Sports Illustrated* Swim . . . .'

'Sold out!'

'Sold out!'

'Last one has just gone bro!'

'AAAAAArrrghhh!'

Onto 5th Avenue, Donald Trump's strip, which plays host to wealthy designer boutiques, ticker tape parades and prime real estate. One nice young lady we speak to sells underpants for $1,000 a pair. But she doesn't sell *Sports Illustrated*.

The Dakota Building is where John Lennon was shot in 1980 and, strangely enough, remains the New York residence of Yoko Ono. A lone security guard patrols the area, and quickly ushers us away when the camera appears. Nigel points to a sign across the road:

'Strawberry Fields. No Littering Please.'

Further up the road, we spot a mosaic that spells out 'Imagine'. The memory of John Lennon lives on.

An actress from Auckland is our host for this evening's outing, and she arrives in a white limo. Tammy has lived in New York for 8 years and is doing her best to follow the American Dream. Her tour of the city begins at the Rainbow Bar at the Rockefeller Building and extravagant cocktails are consumed, before marching into Madison Square Gardens for the NBA clash between the New York Knicks and Milwaukee Bucks. We manage to scab some tickets at US$36 a piece. Typical American razzmatazz – cheerleaders, dancing troupes and fireworks. The Knicks stink, so we leave before the end and hit the sack.

A day of wandering through shops in Soho. The Great American Backrub, Dean and Duluca's, Evolution, Keith Herring's Pop Shop and Liquid Sky. We witness a film in production starring rap star Ice-T. The whole city is a movie, a song and an attitude and it's no more evident than when speaking with the locals.

As one lady quotes: 'If you are paranoid, go with your paranoia.'

Visited Knight Ladernum who had a collection of Eske Monniken photographs of Mexicans. A real eccentric character but very knowledgeable in his chosen field. Stopped for lunch at the Tennessee Mountain Café and absolutely demolished a Mid-Tex Burger – the rest of the crew opt for spare ribs.

Played some basketball with a couple of local children – genuine curiosity regarding the whereabouts of our home country:

'Ain't that some way out by Brazil?'

'No way man. That's like in Canada.'

'Is we right?'

'No. Not even close. It's east of Australia.'

'Where?'

'Ummm, don't bother.'

Bumped into a troupe of singers who sang *When the Cat Came Back*. Joined in but was painfully out of tune.

Back at the hotel, March Madness has taken over. A premiere basketball tournament for the leading universities in the United States, March Madness is being held at Madison Square Gardens this year, and the throng of cheerleaders is testament to the occasion. The odd brass band member strolls through the foyer with instrument strapped to their side.

The ASTA theatre hosts an off Broadway production called *The Blue Men*, a critically acclaimed performance involving three mime artists dressed and painted in blue paint. Bizarre? You bet. It is a hugely entertaining show consisting of various items including fake vomiting, throwing custard, playing musical tubes and toilet paper sculptures. It is an 80-minute whirlwind of a show.

Brooklyn bound. Met up with Marcel who showed us around the Jewish, Polish and Hispanic areas of his 'hood'. He is a screenwriter who lived with Robert Rodriquez (the director of *Desperado*). Another famous bloke is immortalised by his own designer boutique – Spike's Joint is the outlet for trendy neighbourhood streetwear started up by Spike Lee himself.

Like an idiot, I prance around in the trendy attire – for the camera.

Webster Hall is a night club spot that truly rocks. Once we have managed to pass through three different sets of metal detectors and body searches, we move between several floors of manic dance music and scantily clad young ladies. The crew is required to work, shooting Anita and I spiralling through an array of dance moves, and then sit back to enjoy the rest of the evening. Outside, Eddie is patiently waiting.

Howard Stern's radio show wakes me this morning and I realise that I have slept past the call time. Fortunately everybody has done the same so the crew meeting takes place at 'Al's Bakery' round the corner from the Hotel. A chilly wind whisks around the city as Eddie drives us to the

Boyz in d' 'hood.

Helipad for a helicopter ride around the New York Harbour. The chopper gets blown around in the thermals, but still an enjoyable view. Plenty of shots of the Empire State Building and the Statue of Liberty up close.

We need to complete some pickup shots including talking with a cop about life in New York – this has proven to be difficult, all policemen we have encountered have bluntly refused to talk on camera. As luck would have it, we bump into a very friendly Officer Ballew:

'Is it really as violent as we see on television, and in news reports?'

'No, not at all. Most of that happens in minor, isolated incidents around here. Sure, we have violence but you name me one major city in the world that isn't violent in some way?'

'Do you like your job?'

'Well, its kinda like being a lifeguard. 99% boredom, 1% action.'

'But you don't get to work with Pamela Anderson?'

He pulls out his Glock 9mm handgun and truncheon to display. He is surprised to hear that New Zealand policemen are not armed. The only problems we have are lost sheep in the high street.

I run over to a nearby hotdog stand to collect provisions for the boys while Anita is preparing for a ride on a Harley Davidson at the 'American Dream Machine' motorbike store. The trip is taken across the Brooklyn Bridge, and ends up outside the hotel. The city has put on a fabulous day for us, so final shots are taken before we pack our bags. The final few hours of our stay enable me to shop for a number of sports items in the nearby 'Sports Warehouse'.

I ring home to see how the show is rating. It is far exceeding expectations. All the pain and sweat is reaping rewards for everyone involved.

Only 5 days after completing a nightmarish journey halfway around the world, we are about to embark on a similar flight path. Our trip will take us from JFK to Vancouver to Hong Kong to Johannesburg to Cape Town.

This will be our final destination for the first series, so Steve is making sure he has a good time doing it. We all realise that this could be last time we all work together so we are determined to help each other through the difficult few days ahead. All the winter clothing that we have used for Paris and New York has been safely packed into the depths of our suitcases to make way for summer shorts, shirts and thongs.

Africa awaits us.

Chapter 6 | SOUTH AFRICA

Day 37, Monday 10th March

It is 8.30am. The landing gear hitting the tarmac has woken me up. The ordeal of travelling over or through five of the world's continents to get here is almost over, and we wait an hour before boarding the last flight to Cape Town. There is a muggy feel to Cape Town today, and the air is tempered further when two pieces of luggage go missing from our gear count. Thankfully, they are waiting for us at the counter marked 'Oversize' and we collect them.

Meet Rob at the airport and onto our hotel called the V&A. We are pooped by the time we get there but know the demands of a restricted shoot so we need to get on with today's activities. Head straight up to the Noon Gun (an army cannon that fires daily at midday) and we all freak as the gun explodes.

We then make our way to the Noon Gun Café and had a quick bite of Masalha Chicken and Chips and a Vegetarian Dish. The fact that Malay food is served in a Cape Town restaurant is unique but typical of the cosmopolitan feel of the New Republic.

Made our way to the Western Province Stadium in Newlands and visited the rugby Academy – I get the chance to hold the World Cup (William Webb Ellis Trophy – a few dents in it) and then have a run on the Newlands stadium turf.

'The ball swings wide to Eynon. He side-steps Small, through Joubert and past Williams to score a fantastic try.' Oh well, dreams are free.

The Argentinian Under 19 rugby team are also paying a quick visit and I entertain them with a Maori haka to their delight. I have accomplished many things this morning that most people don't even get close to. I have held the World Cup, run onto Newlands and performed a haka in South Africa.

The diamond factory is the next stop – it bores me to tears but Anita finds it quite interesting. We meet Doctor Pinns who talks about the diamond-cutting and their origin. Great talent and a very interesting man – a gemologist.

Our driver for the week is Andy Le Roux, a rugby mad Afrikaans who delights in winding us up about last year's World Cup loss. Despite the playful arguing, he is quite adamant that the All Blacks were the victims of foul play and admits to their superiority.

'You are world leaders when it comes to rugby. No doubt about it'

We wander through downtown Cape Town and pass Nelson Mandela's residence. A truly beautiful building, but he wasn't home. A view of Table Mountain in the setting sun is enough to finish the day with. Despite our lack of sleep, it is decided the best course of action is to hit the town. Hard Rock Café provides a cure for our nourishment and the Sports Café entertainment in the form of video games and live rugby.

Woke to a beautiful day. Clear blue skies and a huge breakfast gave the day a good start. We travel south to the Cape of Good Hope – a big climb to the summit but worthwhile view to greet us at the top. We venture further up to nearby Signal Hill to record the opening shot for the show. Anita and I have both resorted to showing off a bit of leg today – we are both wearing loose clothing and not much of it. Certainly makes a change from our multi-layered winter wear in New York.

The Cape.

A penguin colony is shot followed by a quick boat trip to view a seal colony which is positioned several miles off the Cape Coast. Rough waters but still a real thrill.

The afternoon's journey back enables Roxette to blast out of the van stereo, and a few droopy heads as we sleep on our return to the Hotel. My diaries have suffered in the last few days because of lack of time so I make an effort to add some additional information I quickly fall back to sleep.

An evening outing to Mama Africa's (a famous restaurant) – ate crocodile and sang songs with the kitchen ladies. Some bizarre choices on the menu (kudu, antelope, springbok etc), and everybody is hungry so not much consideration is given to what we eat. The atmosphere was fantastic, and the restaurant is packed. Full stomachs make it easier to fall asleep this evening, not that we have much trouble with that.

I am uneducated when it comes to the art of horse riding but a quick lesson this morning restores my faith in my limited ability. We meet up with Danny and Yvette, two locals who run their own stables. They are

Table Mountain. From left, Rob McLaughlin, Jim, Steve, Nick.

about to undertake a world trip so are interested in plenty of the destinations that we have visited. They are young and enthusiastic – which they'll need to keep for a 3 year trek around the globe.

We break into a soft canter, and then a gallop which I am frightened to death of. A second gallop was fine. I felt like I was bouncing down a motorway on my bare bum. Anita has Cassie, while I have Tequila. The horseriding happens at Chapmand's Bay where, coincidentally, the wreck of the Kakapo lies to rest. It was completing a trip from England to New Zealand when it ran aground on its maiden voyage.

We return to the stables and then make our way to the Bungee Rocket – sadly no-one is there but a quick stroll down the Clifton Beach compensates. Plenty of golden sand and equally golden bodies. The water, however, is absolutely freezing.

The schedule has been disrupted so we move onto the Cape Bird Sanctuary and I take the opportunity to have a chat to our intrepid guide, Andy Le Roux. His view of the country is an interesting one and he says that the culture shock due to the breaking down of apartheid is apparent. Blacks and Whites now work and socialise together but rarely live, marry or date each other – the cultures and lifestyles are so different that he predicts it may take 3 or 4 generations before attitudes change and cohesion exists. There has been plenty of hardship on the way, but all heading to a better place.

On the road to Stellenbosch and a visit to Brampton Wineries, run by Rodney – a Kiwi gent who has mastered the art of wine-making and is now mixing it with the best vineyards in Southern Africa. Anita conducts the interview while I muck around with the wine-vats. I open the valve of one huge tanker and it gets sprayed all over my face. The force of the wine hurts my eyes but it's a classic moment.

Our hotel tonight is called Lanzarec, beautiful rooms but I found an enormous bug in my room. Ordered a huge sandwich from room service and then reflected on the day. The weather has been pleasant and I am mildly sunburnt.

It seems as if the moment I put my head to the pillow, my alarm blurts out a wake-up call. It is 5.30am and in two hours time we are flying to Johannesburg.

On landing, we quickly transfer to Phoodspreit. Arrived to meet Malek who drives one and a half hours to get to Makalali Lodge – we pick

And how would sir like his wildebeest?

up Pax and Rudolf (additional guides) – and are then greeted by Chris and the Lodge attendants at our final destination.

The camp site is pretty amazing (reminds me of the tree forts from the Ewoks movie) Pinewood tied together with a pool, viewing platform and outdoor shower with a toilet. We are all incredibly impressed. The lunch consists of lentil soup, bread and roasted vegetables plus rice.

Jonathan took us out to look at the animals (my first safari), saw a lioness and cub plus a sprinkling of elephants. They look aggressive and untamed – different to the ones in India. The jeep goes over some lumpy ground but is smooth due to the awesome suspension. Raymond is our tracker and is very good.

After viewing, we stopped on an elevated hill and drank orange juice and ate botang. The silence is almost deafening with the exception of cicadas and birds.

Returned to a banquet of rump, Algerian chicken and small potatoes, beans and fruit salads to finish. A great spread and good company. The servants have extraordinary names, Godswill, Killer and Benji. We are trying to delay our flight so that we can stay a few extra days.

Wild animal safari.

An early start for another safari trip. The weather is overcast but extremely pleasant. We venture out and spot giraffes. Two young ones who look scared. We then find a big giraffe that runs off – looks like a slow motion replay. Our tracker Ray is brilliant at spotting tracks. He spots a grass snake about 30 metres away.

Spot two rhinos. The pup weighs about 40 kgs but the mother is huge. They don't seem to be too worried about the presence of the jeep. You almost feel guilty for disturbing their territory. Just enough time to spot a zebra and stop for morning tea.

A quick breakfast and then bid farewell to Makalali. Our mammoth trip back to New Zealand starts today. I am so annoyed that we don't have time to stick around for more action. The week has been too quick, I haven't even had time to write much in my diary – simply because there has been no time.

Thankfully, we have the last show in the can. The first series is finished and we can all spend a few months with our feet firmly on the ground.

DESTINATION ANYWHERE

Chapter 7 | WALES

Day 42, Saturday 9th August

It's the first day of the new series shoot and I find myself just 10 miles outside of Oxford. Fair play if we had decided to film in this university city, but the call sheet says Cardiff, and, ultimately, I need to get there before 3pm. Word from home is that the crew will not arrive until early afternoon from Gatwick so, for once, it won't be necessary to rush my journey.

My alarm throws me out of a deep sleep and into the throngs of concerted panic as I desperately try to remember every travel detail I had meticulously planned the previous night.

'Where the hell is my passport?'

'I'm sure I left my ticket in this pocket?'

Sadly, even the most organised individual can be a terrible traveller, and I manage to be bad at both. Oxford to Cardiff is a comfortable journey on a map but, in reality, it requires a taxi, bus, train and another taxi to reach the biggest city in the Land of Leeks and Laverbread. The journey on British Rail takes me from the golden, maize fields of the west country through Bristol, Newport and into the Welsh capital.

Two elderly men strike up the inevitable conversation:

'Wales? Pah! If there's one thing our national team excel at . . .' starts one.

'. . . it's playing like a crock of complete shite,' adds the other.

'But *your* boys – well, in a completely different league, they are.'

'That Colin Meads was a hard bugger wasn't he, eh?'

'He's not still playing is he?'

'No, it's that Zipzap Brooke that's the flavour, innit?'

God, it's like watching Morcombe and Wise.

The scenery change from England to Wales is nothing drastic, but the transformation in weather is encouraging as the cloud dissipates into deep blue sky as we enter the Principality.

'Lincoln House Hotel, please!' I tell my taxi driver, who leads me into the heart of the city. Our hotel is on Cathedral Road, which plays host to a colossal number of guest houses and runs perpendicular to the main road of Cardiff. The usual weekend crush of tourists is intensified by the fact that the 'Big Weekend Festival' – one of the largest music and entertainment gatherings in the United Kingdom – is in its final throes.

My driver is rather concerned about the brewing undertones of the 'Asian Festival' – also held in these first few weeks of August. According to local news reports, several hundred members of the British National Front arrived last night at the train station and have since gone 'underground'. They are well known for their racist marches and their presence is causing angst.

'They're always causing bloody trouble. It's no good for tourism, you know.' he says in his Welsh sing-song manner, 'We need someone like Jonah to sort 'em out, ha, ha, ha.'

'You're probably right,' I chime.

'No. I am right.'

The Hotel takes the form of a re-furbished Victorian house with its original features and atmosphere, although most rooms have modern en-suite facilities. The house assistant, Pat, attends to my needs straight away by thrusting a bunch of bananas in my face, insisting that I need to put on weight:

'Aye laddie. Ye look too thin,' she cracks in a Scottish accent.

I settle into my room by gobbling every free biscuit in sight, and calling in to visit the crew. Cameron, our Australian sound-man, has already found a local café to attack a coffee, while Steve 'Ors' Orsbourn unpacks his camera gear and our director Rob MacLaughlin confirms arrangements by phone.

It also gives me a chance to catch up with this week's guest presenter Belinda Todd, who is looking remarkably fresh and composed after a 27 hour flight from Auckland. Rob informs us the afternoon is

Brown's Hotel in Wales: home of the bed of Dylan Thomas

free, so I venture into town in search of culture, ambience, and a pub to watch the weekend's Tri-Nations game.

In all truth, Cardiff does not dazzle visually, nor does it project any real historical brilliance, but in the summer sun the colours seem brighter, the people browner and, as I stroll down Westgate Street towards the main shopping complex, I feel that there are plenty worse places to be. To my right, I notice a bulky and rather hideous concrete structure, that seems to be decaying at the foundations and almost falling over. To my surprise, I pass a billboard displaying the reconstruction plan of this lifeless 'eye-sore' titled 'The National Stadium – Home of Welsh Rugby'. I chuckle at the irony in the comparison of their stadium with the current state of their national game. Crap.

Belinda Todd and Nick Eynon.

The stadium was due to be finished by next June but, typically, construction has been delayed and there seems to be a fear that it will only be completed a few weeks before the World Cup is due to kick off in October 1999.

At 7.00pm we gather outside the nearby Coopers field and head towards the 'Big Weekend' Summer Festival which is heading into its busiest period. The action is based at Cathays Park – only a five minute walk from the hotel- and it is already heaving with action when we arrive. There are food and game stalls, merry-go-rounds and roller coasters, and a huge sound stage pumping out various jungle and trance dance tracks, like a true town fair. Free entry guarantees a full turnout and we are amazed at the number of people who are swarming through the gates – in particular the eligible young women. I am eager to try the rides and opt for 'The Swing Boat' which acts as a pendulum ride, propelling keen 'thrill enthusiasts' at ridiculous speeds until they are ill. It works. Rob and I remain wobbly-legged for the rest of the night.

'Can we go on that now? Please? Can we go on this?'

I am beginning to sound like a kid in a candy store.

After a shot at Rifle Range and winning Belinda a teddy bear, we sit back and watch the fireworks while the Chemical Brothers reverberate from the sound stage. I grab an Indian takeaway and fall asleep with the Chemical Brothers still thumping in my ears.

A cool, crisp morning. The chaos and exciting atmosphere from last night has transformed itself into a pristine calm. We are not filming until midday so, in order to clear out the cobwebs, I jog around the local park. We meet with our Tourist Board representative, Rhiann, at midday who informs us that 'The Big Weekend' finishes tonight with an outdoor concert by London artist 'Omar' starting around 9.00pm. The schedule is changed to incorporate this option.

Our transport for the week appears in the form of a blue Accord and an Escort van – quickly dubbed 'The Plumber's Wheels'. We take the main road north through Mountain Ash into the sleepy hollow of Crickhowell and stop at The Bear Hotel – a classic village pub which doubles up as a hotel and an ideal place to stop for a few nights.

Cam McGrath outside the Haycastle Bookshop, Wales

Traditional leek soup is consumed before we hit the road north through the rugged valley territory passing Ebbw Vale and the Black Mountains to the village of Hay-on-Wye. With over 35 bookstores, this tiny village is better known as 'The Town of Books', and the Castle and High Streets play host to most of them including The Children's Bookrooms, The Book Warehouse, The Poetry Bookshop, Bohemian Books, Rare Comics and the specially featured Honesty Bookstore – a unique display of literature that harbours no price tags or payment counter. You simply deposit several coins or notes into a collection box and walk off with your purchase. Sadly, in my opinion, the books are either too thick or too old to generate any real interest but the lads giggle over the humorously titled 'Big Dix'.

DESTINATION ANYWHERE

'Have you got any comics?' I ask an elderly gentleman. His stare is cold. I leave.

As it happens, we have visited Hay-on-Wye during a quiet period, but are reliably informed that during the Book Festival (as if Wales needs more festivals!) the village attracts collectors from around the world. I have noticed that the presence of the camera doesn't bother the locals unduly, and guess that they have plenty of media visits throughout the year.

From "Big Dix" to "Three Cocks".

My watch reads 4.35pm, but the sun blazes down with midday ferocity and Rhiann becomes 'Goddess of the Day' when she returns with four ice cold mineral waters. Our final task at the Town of Books is to pop into the supposed largest bookstore in the world, Richard Booths, which sits on Lion Street and is guarded by a gnarly figure straight from *Bad Jelly the Witch*. The sign inside the door states: 'Books Constantly Purchased – Any Quantity, Anywhere, Anytime. Europe's Largest Secondhand Bookshop.' There is no mention of being the world's largest, so we assume Rhiann is a notorious liar. There are over 400,000 books spread over two stories, ranging from crime to sci-fi, sex manuals to sports biographies. No purchases.

We wave goodbye to 'Bad Jelly' and travel into the welcoming arms of the Upper Trewalkin Bed and Breakfast – only ten minutes out of Hay and up several narrow country roads. Cam, who is driving the 'Plumber', is convinced a combine harvester is going to hit us, but we arrive safely and our host, Maydwyn, stuffs our faces with tea and Welsh cakes to ease growing hunger pangs.

The B & B is a cheaper and more relaxed alternative to a city hotel, and Upper Trewalkin is the archetypal guest house for tourists who enjoy the open air of the Valleys. The house is large and warm, with the bleating of sheep being the only audible hazard, and the rooms are typically cozy. Maydwyn assures us that the personal touch that accompanies the B & B is the true difference, although charging only a tenth of the cost of a large hotel is proof enough.

She anticipates that the Rugby World Cup in 1999 will attract copious amounts of visitors to her abode, and is already preparing for the onslaught by purchasing another property. Her bouncy manner warms us all, and the crew struggle to remain composed in the pristinely kept surroundings as Cam almost breaks every piece of crockery in the living room while trying to pour a cup of tea.

We return to Cardiff to find the crowds overflowing from Cathays Park as Omar plays to an assiduous crowd of varying age in the grand finale of 'The Big Weekend'.

We are on our way out of the city, westbound, by 8.30am and I consume the last of Pat's bananas for breakfast. It is the coolest part of the day and the chill whisks through the open window, but according to the Manchurian tones of the breakfast host on the radio:

'You've woken up to the British Summer. It should be over by five o'clock!'

Oakwood Leisure Centre sits in the county of Pembrokeshire, ninety minutes west of the capital, and is our first port of call today. It is a manufactured theme park that, according to the Internet, boasts the best rollercoaster in the world, and is set in an 'environmentally friendly' enclosure. In other words, they've kept the trees.

Our media representative, Simon (who looks too young to be the

---

Belinda at Oakwood. The rollercoaster is behind the trees.

assistant marketing director) explains how Oakwood endeavours to portray a family atmosphere by keeping the rides simple and enjoyable. The site boasts over 30 food stalls, a roller coaster, numerous fun rides and picnic areas that are spread generously over the farming estate. We notice that Simon's position of authority enables us to jump the far-reaching queues, as well as generating adoring smiles from his female work colleagues, and he is quite comfortable carrying some of our extra equipment.

The imposing Vertigo ride haunts the horizon like a derelict series of pylons, and judging from the series of hysterical screams, I correctly predict two things:

1. This is Oakwood's 'piece de resistance'
2. I have to ride it.

A horse-shoe shaped structure stands perpendicular to a 130 foot tower, connected by a number of wire cords that act as a huge pendulum weight with the 'punters' harnessed to the swinging cradle. The result is a 40 foot freefall before the weight is taken by the wire cords and the Vertigo swings into action. Before long, Belinda and I are strapped in and winched up to the launching point, where we both play out important roles. She pulls the rip-cord while I hold the digital camera. The freefall forces my stomach to squeeze out my ears, but the resulting swing sends a rush of adrenalin through the veins and we both scream our lungs to full capacity.

'My stomach is coming out my mouth!' I manage to scream. I can't hear what Belinda is saying, she could be throwing up for all I know.

Rob informs us that a second drop is needed for filming purposes, so we relive the experience and knock another ten years off our life expectancy. Watching the crew have a go prompts the biggest laugh of the morning. Cam and Steve are both bulky lads and each stand over six foot three, while Rob eats his fair share of pies so the combined weight gives the swing so much momentum that the Vertigo almost performs a full revolution. And then some.

Simon whisks us onto the most popular attraction at Oakwoods, the Megaphobia Roller Coaster, which already has a two hundred metre long queue of anxious but excited children with equally animated parents. Simon explains that Megaphobia was voted 'best roller coaster in the world' by the Internet only last year, and has been inundated with

American tourist companies who plan 'thrill excursions'. The structure is traditionally wooden with a number of hair pin turns, and is guaranteed not to give you the same ride twice – something a metal ride is unable to do. The ride takes only 25 seconds, but is extremely exhilarating. Poor Steve has to try and film us while sitting backwards on the front seat. Glamorous job, huh?

'Stay still, would you?' he shouts, as we pass through a gravity defying loop.

Llangharne is a small village in Carmarthen Bay, and is the place where literary giant Dylan Thomas wrote and lived with his wife. Belinda investigates his old living abode while I take time to visit Brown's Hotel, a local pub where Thomas' bed was given to publican Tom Watts. He still keeps it upstairs and has recently been embroiled in a row with Dylan Thomas' daughter for the rights to ownership. As it was a gift, Tom is reluctant to let it go.

The pub is full of local characters who remind us that the All Blacks were beaten by Llanelli in 1972, and are fast to point the camera in the direction of the team photo on the wall. Like most places in Wales, you are always hard pressed to win an argument about rugby, but I can't help feeling that the older generation are still living in the past glories instead of appreciating the modern game. Anyway, that is another argument.

The afternoon sun drifts slowly out of sight as we head to the CyberCafe back on Castle Street in Cardiff. The CyberCafe is the new communication trend whereby a small sum is paid to collect and send e-mail on the Internet. Costing you three pounds for thirty minutes, you are able to keep in touch with friends, business contacts and family at the touch of a button. Cam finds a job offer, while Rob finds the *Christchurch Press* on line to prove the success rate.

The day over, I take time to write my diary and go for a run. The Topp Twins appear on television as part of the Edinburgh Festival celebrations and, in typical boisterous fashion, cause presenter Mark Lamarr countless problems with their unpredictable personalities. Despite the home grown entertainment, I fall asleep.

A fax from home delivers the news that we fly out to Florence on Friday, resulting in the loss of a shooting day this week. This prompts Rob to make a few small adjustments to the timetable, and Cardiff Castle becomes the priority this morning.

The Castle has a history spanning almost two thousand years, and has been passed through the hands of many noble families, until finally during the 18th century it became the property of the Marquis of Bute. The Butes were largely responsible for the industrial development of Cardiff, which transformed it from a small town into a major national port.

As part of the tour we are shown into the largest room in the Castle, the Banqueting Hall, which displays lavish carvings and murals each telling the stories of medieval Lords. The Hall is still used for Royal and Civic occasions and can be hired out to the public for only 150 pounds a head. I take off my shoes and 'sock-ski' my way down the polished floor. Belinda gives me a disgusted look. We wander into the Private Chapel, the Roof Garden and look over the Castle Green, which contains historic remains from the Roman and Medieval period.

There are, like the Tower of London, resident Castle birds that take the form of arrogant peacocks – who bluntly refuse to unfeather their fantastic tails – until a small Spanish child begins to kick one around the courtyard, prompting a major incident with the Castle tour guides.

A visit to the traditional Welsh beer specialists, Brain's Brewery, prompts a cheerful look from the crew while I take time to wander

---

Travel tip: avoid TV crews when touring.

downtown in search of some talcum powder to fix a nasty rash that has appeared on my backside after jogging earlier in the week. There is a universal linguistic affinity with the word 'arse' which means I have no problem conveying the information to the local pharmacists. Smiles all round.

On my return, I discover that Brain's have offered to pay for our lunch and we all heartily tuck into a feast of chicken burgers and pasta slops. When it comes to alcohol, I would qualify as the world's worst authority, so Rob thinks it only fair that Belinda should conduct the interview and taste the local brew with Brains representative Lousie Prynne – who has gone up in our estimations due to the free lunch. Frantic looks in the direction of his wristwatch indicates that Rob wants to move on so we say our goodbyes.

At 3.30 in the afternoon, our little convoy arrives at Llancaiach Fawr – the site of the country's only Natural Living Museum. It really is a step back in time, as the guides all dress in traditional 1645 authentic attire and, even more impressively, speak in 17th century tongue.

We are immediately thrust into the action with a falconry and owl display before Bleddyn (our hosed and buckled guide) takes us on a tour of the house. He is unflappable in his role and while it is difficult to understand his dialect at times, (he is an inspiring actor) his dedication to the cause is impressive. While he must be tempted to talk rugby or girls, he continues to address me as 'my lord' and Belinda as 'my lady' although at the end of the working week he proclaims his weakness for 'getting heartily pissed'.

Two pieces of good news this morning. Firstly, my rash has cleared due to the heavy application of talcum powder. Secondly, Pat has offered to do my washing instead of lumbering it to the local, and rather dodgy, laundromat. We load up the cars and I continue to torment Cam with my choice of music in the car stereo. He threatens to deliberately crash the car if he hears Coolio for the hundredth time.

The direction is east to Caerleon which is the home to the ancient Roman Baths, ancient ruins, the legendary birthplace of King Arthur, and Doctor Russell Rees, an expert on architecture and the history of the Round Table, who carefully and passionately narrates some fantastic stories. To go with his wealth of information, he also possesses a collection of wooden chairs – grotesque faces and images carved into pine trunks – one of which is supposed to squeak when sat on by a virgin. It doesn't work. Or at least, doesn't squeak.

Chepstow Castle lies on the banks of the River Wye, only a stone's throw from England. It was the site of some Welsh resistance to the English advances some years ago but serves as one of the most visited tourist sites in the country. Its sturdy walls and rugged stone work cast a formidable shadow on the Gwent landscape.

Boredom, thy name is sightseeing.

By the time we get to Tintern Abbey, another decaying ruin, I have had enough of looking at castles. It sounds coarse and unsympathetic but you can only absorb so much history and culture in one day. It is 5.00pm on the sixth day and my cup hath run over. The Abbey is, nevertheless, impressive with its high stone surroundings cutting a majestic silhouette in the early evening sun. The return trip is spent dozing in the front seat.

By 8.00pm we are sitting outside the 'Boar's Head' pub with Euros Wynn, a South Welshman who was once a presenter with the Welsh television channel S4C, but now is an associate producer with his own production company. He talks about the Welsh language and its role in today's society (S4C is a Welsh language channel). The interview is unique considering he has never appeared on screen speaking English, and we take the opportunity to test our linguistic skills. He teaches us the basic lessons: the 'th' pronunciation of 'dd' in Pontypridd, and 'thl' of 'Ll' in Llanelli. (It is difficult enough saying it, let alone printing it!)

Interestingly enough, due to New Zealand's isolation, we are a nation of imitators, and the 'DPE' crew have spent a large part of the week testing our accents on Rhiann and Beth, a new guide who has joined the trip. This has led to a rather pathetic 'renaming' process that sees Cam, Steve, Rob and Nick replaced by 'Gareth', 'Llewwllyn', 'Arwel' and 'Bevan'. Pathetic, really.

There is always a need to capture nightlife on film, so we haul our weary hides to Club ifor Bach – one of the busiest hot spots in town that tonight, for some reason, is neither hot or busy. The club is split into three stories – light metal, Britpop and hard-core dance. Belinda and I almost fall asleep on each other, so Rob pulls the pin at midnight and we call it quits for the day.

At bed at one, up at six, showered and shaved by seven, on the road by eight-thirty. We are heading west to the Swansea markets which enjoy their most popular custom on Thursdays and Fridays – hence its re-scheduling from Monday to today. The market is set inside what looks like a deserted airport hanger – vast and repulsively designed but strangely warm and welcoming. We are here to taste the local delicacy – Welsh cockles and laverbread – and pave our way through the traditional fruit and vegetable stands towards the fish displays.

Cathy and Simone prepare our breakfast while entertaining us with the stories of the morning's catch. The cockles are locally acquired from the Swansea Bay but, during lean periods, also acquired from Scottish waters. Judging from the aging photos on the walls the business has been passed down the generations and Cathy describes the long, laborious hours involved in making a living out of seafood. The men catch, while the women sell and cook. It's a hard life but they are equally happy.

Laverbread does not resemble bread at all. It represents a type of seaweed, also dragged up from the seabed and, when cooked, tastes of warm wall paper paste. We are told that the locals eat it by the bucket full, and I am determined to put on a brave face when forcing it down.

'So what do you think then?' she asks.

'Hmmm, yummy?' I reply, looking like a bulldog chewing wasps.

It's bloody horrible and tastes like cold porridge.

Cathy heats the cockles, while Simone heats the boiled laverbread in the oil of Welsh bacon. All three are served together, and I am pleasantly surprised. At how horrible it really is.

On the tip of Swansea Bay lies a Port Eynon, a small fishing village that carries my surname. Every since I was a young boy, I was often told of my Welsh roots and how the name originated from these parts. Although I have no direct blood relations in this part of the world, it is strange to be able to pick up the local phone book and see 'Eynon' as common as 'Smith'. Feeling every bit the conquering hero, I head to Pontypridd.

Rob has left the best bit until last as I walk into the red bricked crafthouse that plays host to the 'Grogg Shop' – a collection of the most famous sporting caricature statues in the world. John Hughes and son Richard have become world renown for making lifelike clay models of various personalities ranging from rugby players Jonah Lomu, Neil Jenkins and Nick Farr-Jones to soccer stars Bobby Charlton and Ryan

Giggs. The shop is an open shrine to some of the best sportsmen in living memory and the memorabilia is just as astounding.

Richard shows the lads behind the scenes while I talk with John about the merits of his business. Luciano Pavarotti was his last client, despite the fact that it took 8 weeks to complete a little 'Luci'.

At the conclusion, he offers us a choice of player and naturally we all jump towards the All Black shelf. I get Sean Fitzpatrick, Jonah finds a friend in Steve and Rob gladly entertains the 12 inch John Kirwan.

When dawn breaks, it's a designated day of travel and, to fuel up for the journey, I inform Pat that I will be having a cooked breakfast for the first time this week. She celebrates my indulgence by constructing the largest bacon buttie in living history while simultaneously presenting my laundry – washed and ironed from early in the week. Legend.

We lock and load and hit the road early but the morning traffic is still heavy on the M4 to London. The cars take us to Gatwick, and within two hours we are sitting on Flight IG 3538 Meridiana Airways to Florence. Winding our clocks forward we arrive at 5.45pm, and I almost fall over when told by the stewardess that the early evening temperature has dropped by two degrees. To 38°C.

Chapter 8 | Italy

Day 49, Saturday 16th August

Florence lies in the Northern territories of Italy, in the province of Tuscany, and is only eighty kilometres from the Western Coast of the Ligurian Sea. The region is populated largely with vineyards and sunflower fields while the city plays host to some of the most significant art and sculpture collections on earth. A quick look out my window reveals a clay-coloured landscape, sparsely dotted with greenery, while the simmering heat distorts the view in its relentless madness.

Seeing the heat is one thing. Feeling it is another.

The airport does not come fully assembled, and we need to complete the walk from our plane to the terminal without the assistance of a covered tunnel. The heat off the tarmac is stifling, although we wonder how it must feel during the midday sun as opposed to this early evening 'whimper'.

My last visit to Italy was during our Rome shoot in December of last year, and I was suitably impressed with the laid back casual demeanour of the Italians. Despite their occasional fiery emotive outbursts, their overwhelming desire to make the day move as slowly as possible is admirable. The Italian appreciation for the finer things in life – wine, food, sleep, women (or men) – far outweighs any characteristic flaws. However, even my patience is tested when we discover only ONE customs official in charge of stamping over two hundred passports.

Hotel De La Ville is only twenty minutes out of the airport and positioned in the Piazza Antinori, which seems to be central to everything. Our researchers have done well in choosing accommodation, the rooms are spacious and I have two toilets – or at least I think they're two toilets. The receptionist is an Italian beauty: long brown hair, deep dark eyes and lips that would melt a snowman in seconds. Sadly, she's as grumpy as a tired grandmother and does a superb Oscar the Grouch.

We meet up with Mark Everton, this week's director, Dave Collins, our researcher (who travels to Amsterdam tomorrow) and Marie Theresa, our tour guide. Mark has set up an interview for tonight, so it is a quick change and back into the van before we have time to settle in properly.

The streets are a buzz with activity, although we are told by Marie Theresa that the nightlife is very subdued in Florence – nightclubs are non-existent, so I assume the activity is generated through cafes and restaurants. The chance of meeting a local girl is also fairly remote, as the native Firenze population all migrate to the coast during the summer, and I am wondering what chances we have of seeing any action.

I am wearing my 'smart' change of clothes – only reserved for the most upmarket occasions – which are causing me to sweat prolifically. My nylon long sleeve shirt is already soaking but, thanks to its light colour, it is hardly detected.

We arrive at 14 Via de' Bardi, home of Lorenzo Villoresi, one of most adored perfume makers in Europe. His work has included personal scents for the late Jackie Kennedy Onassis and super model Linda Evangelista, and now he is going to attempt to impress Sir Nicholas 'Maori Bloke' Eynon. I scan over some of the information that Mark has obtained from the Tourist Board:

'Lorenzo Villoresi's laboratory, located amid the rooftops of Florence, practices the art of perfumery. He combined his Tuscan heritage with the knowledge of the science of perfumery and with extensive travelling throughout the Middle East, to create an original line of perfumery, essences, lotions and other products for the body and the home.'

Lorenzo proceeds to construct a blueprint of fragrances that he feel reflects my personality. He quizzes me on smells and senses from my youth and I can only weakly reply: 'Some thing earthy and floral?' – reminders of rugby fields and fishing at Days Bay as a nipper. After mixing and concocting like some demented sorcerer, he presents me with the final product, encased in a dark blue lead crystal bottle. I immediately test my 'scent' on the crew, who all agree that Lorenzo has done a fine job. He then files my handiwork and we are all treated to orange juice and sugar bread, while overlooking the dimming lights of Firenze from the vantage point of Lorenzo's 13th century patio.

Marie Theresa talks fondly of the Villoresi family – one of the few Italian aristocratic clans that we have access to – and informs us that

Lorenzo and his wife are departing tomorrow for New York on business. We leave and I hold my perfume bottle close, like a kid with a new toy.

'If you don't want it, I'll have it!' shouts Cam.

Six times out of the last seven nights, I have slept soundly. I set my alarm to wake me at 5.00am but I oversleep by an hour. I ring home to find that the All Blacks have won a scrappy encounter with the Aussies 36-24, and, following a European-style breakfast of ham, bread, fruit and juice, I manage to catch the rugby highlights on CNN.

My phone rings:

'Did you see the rugby? The boys won, the boys won!' Steve's familiar tones.

'I saw it. Shall we have a beer to celebrate?'

'It's 6.15am!'

'I know.'

Pause.

'Okay.'

Mark has a meeting with some Tourist Board officials so Steve, myself and Cam venture out to get familiar with the narrow alleyways and streets of Florence. I experiment with my 'aroma' on a number of young ladies who seem to share the opinion that the perfume is beautiful and fresh, but were not keen to take it any further than that. Not that I was pushing it. Honest.

I come across an Australian who seems keen enough:

'Do you speak English?'

'Yeah.'

'Have a whiff of this.' I thrust my perfume under her nose, 'Whadda ya think?'

'Oh, it's quite nice.'

'So, shall we go out on a date then?'

'No.'

'Why not?'

'Cause I don't like you.'

Charmed, I'm sure.

Due to a jumbo dose of luck, Mark has managed to secure four window tickets to the annual Palio horse race in Siena this afternoon, so our driver Fabrizio negotiates the bumpy highway south to get us there on time. In hindsight, I must have looked quite disinterested when told we were going to the races – done it before at Trentham, and lost money. This race, however, is like no other.

The Palio is the most exhilarating and aggressive horse race that you will ever see. It also seems to be a way of life. The jockeys race for the rival districts of Siena, known as the Contrada. The city has 17 different Contrada who represent the last remaining regiments of the city republic's medieval army. Some of the alliances and rivalries date back hundreds of years, and their lives revolve around the horse race.

No-one outside of the city seems to fully understand the way Siena works or what happens to its people in the four day buildup to the scariest horse race in the world. Bespectacled bank clerks will abruptly leave good sense behind to demolish heads and crush testicles, while sweet-faced old ladies howl like 19-year-old maniacs when their horse appears from its heavily guarded stables. Teenage girls claw at themselves in horror if their horse looks lame. Behind the scenes, old men, the Contrade gaffers, the Godfathers, strike deals and plan vendettas.

On the day of the race itself, in its two minute run, jockeys are encouraged to whip one another, limbs are broken, horses can die and egos are always destroyed.

We are told that the real danger of the race wasn't in its running. It was the losing. Come in second and the likelihood is that your supporters will give you a whipping you'll never forget. Better to come in third or even last. Second guarantees you a spanking.

The rules are weird enough to give the NZRFU nightmares. The big problem lies in the way things are done. To begin with you don't actually pick your own horse, it's chosen by lots. So is your position on the start line, where the violence of the race comes into play. If the horse is a born loser, then your Contrada will instruct you to do a deal with your adversaries – bribes in other words.

After shuffling through the frantic masses, we are led upstairs of an aging apartment block to our own window box. The sight of the heaving thousands below is astonishing, and we wait in eager anticipation.

As the horses appear, the crowd start cheering 'I dieci assassini' (the contract killers) which is the universal chant for the jockeys. While they line themselves at the start, I overhear a conversation between two spectators in the next row:

'Who are you supporting?' says one man.

'Contrada Del Bruno,' the other replies.

'Any chance of your rider selling himself on the line?'

'If he did,' the man smiles, 'we'd beat him to death with sticks. It's a luxury he can't permit himself.'

After seven excruciating false starts, the starting gun erupts into life and all hell breaks loose. One horse has already lost its rider and is heading round the track in the wrong direction. Another rider has been tossed beneath angry hooves, and another dobbin hasn't moved from the start line. Before you know it, the three minute race has passed in three seconds, and it's over. A deafening explosion signals the end. All at once, the crowds spill over the barriers. Fights erupt and I see men and women crying. In all the hype, I don't even notice who won – the guy in red, I think.

The celebrations carry on into the night, while our intrepid team try to come back down to earth. Slowly. By the way, the La Giraffa won.

The event has been spectacular and we travel back in good spirits. Lynette Forday has slept almost the whole day and has recovered from her jet lag. After a wash-up, Steve and I wander down town to a small pizza restaurant for a quick feed.

The church across the road from the hotel is closed this morning. It has been open all week but shuts its mammoth doors on Sunday. Strange.

Lynette is keen to get a good look around. She is bitterly disappointed that the perfumery and Palio have happened during her absence. Today will provide some compensation as we drive to the Medici Chappelen – the private chapel of the wealthy Medici family, which is open to public viewing. So rich and influential were the family that they commissioned Michelangelo to provide the interior sculptures and paintings.

Some of the outstanding Florentine designs are characteristic of his work, but perhaps more fascinating are the number of unfinished statues that have been placed inside the chapel dome. Marie-Theresa (our guide) explains that artist will toil over a statue for several years, decide the proportions were incorrect and then refuse to complete the work.

Strolled the streets in search of the famed Duomo, the enormous dome on top of the city cathedral, and discovered it. It makes a great reference point in case you get lost amid the endless cobblestone streets.

'It's almost like Italy's equivalent of the Sky Tower.'

'No, it's not. It's nothing like an oversized penis.'

Michelangelo Square provides an ideal place to enjoy a sweeping view of the city, and Lynette has time to chat to a street painter called Andreas. The breath-taking landscape leaves no shortage of inspiration for any artist. His watercolour creations reflect the exquisite beauty of this ancient city, but his prices reflect a shrewd businessman. A lunch break is called before Steve and I head off to the local swimming baths in search of nice angles and skimpy bikinis.

Mark's partner, Marcia, and daughter Holly have beaten us there, and have already swum, showered and changed before we step through the doors. Walking among the brown-bodied and dark featured Italians we both stick out like sore thumbs – so we make a concerted effort to hide the camera equipment. Eyes scrutinise and heads turn, making me more uncomfortable so we abandon any thought of capturing the locals on film and sit back on our deck chairs and admire the view.

From a male perspective, the Italian women seem to have real attitude and a certain snobbish persona but there's no denying their beauty and confidence. I get to further my female education as I wander around town with Cameron, and spot various beauties in their natural habitat before turning in. Alone.

The room service prices are ridiculously high. A simple burger is going to set me back around NZ$20.00. Although it's always the easy option, room service is the most expensive way of eating. This hotel has a restaurant that cooks the food and then delivers it straight to your door in a matter of minutes. Although the prices are ridiculous, I order a full fruit salad and french fries.

The Medici family owned a number of significant landmarks in Florence. Their own private chapel, museum, monument and . . . er . . . torture chamber. Dating back to 1066, this crumbling prison once echoed with the dying screams of enemies and criminals who perished in various tortuous ways. Decaying iron handcuffs and metal racks line the concrete walls, and various prison-related trinkets are displayed in viewing cabinets.

We shoot various angles and record a piece about Stendahl's Syndrome – a condition of fatigue and disorientation created through the over-exposure to fine art. I know it sounds ridiculous, but it was discovered that the average tourist finds it difficult to view more than two galleries a day. Symptoms include weariness, boredom and disinterest.

The Ponte Vecchio, Florence.

Stendahl's Syndrome gets the chance to rear it's ugly head at our first gallery stop, The Ufizzi. This four storey building contains the best work of Michelangelo, and we are also treated to a rare viewing of a secret chamber of work that is closed to the general public. The work includes several dark creations from the artist incorporating various horrific images of murder and suicide. During the war, this private passage was partially destroyed by a German bomb – shrapnel pock-marks on the walls are visual evidence of this attack. We convey our gratitude to the caretaker and he locks the door. For another ten years I suppose.

The Italian food is proving popular with the TV crew, and the rather unadventurous choice of pizza is repeated for lunch. Nearby the Ponte Vecchio bridge connects the East and West banks of the city, and is the city's most famous landmark. Tradesmen proclaim their bargains, while love-struck teenagers cradle each other on the clay-coloured stone, as the Ponte becomes the ideal place for us to snap some publicity photographs.

Yesterday, we were unable to gain entry to the Accodemia Museum but Marie-Theresa has been successful in her application and we waltz through its hallowed gates at 1.00pm. The Accodemia is home to the

Statue of David – arguably the most famous sculptured image in the world – and the first glimpse of its magnificence proves to be rather humbling. The proportion is remarkable and it seems to glow in the afternoon light, as we all look bug-eyed upon the awesome defeater of Goliath.

'What's he standing on?' I ask Marie Theresa.

'Uneven ground. Which is what he was modelled on,' she replies.

'In most modern paintings, David is pictured with his foot raised atop the body of Goliath, which is a morbid image. This is the way he should be portrayed,' she says pointing at the Statue.

A magnificent example of manhood: Michelangelo's David with cherubim Nick and "Dr Kwan, Medicine Woman" Lynette Forday.

Stendahl's Syndrome is kicking in and, before it debilitates us completely, Mark insists we visit the Villa Villaresi – a private hotel run by the sister of Lorenzo – and swim in the warm water of their heated pool. We watch the immense sun sink into the romantic landscape from the luxury of our poolside deck chairs.

On the road again, as Fabrizio packs the van with our luggage and the highway trip to Siena begins in the early hours. Fabrizio is a tireless worker whose mobile phone never stops ringing during the day, and we predict a lovestruck girlfriend is responsible for the calls. He can't speak fluent English but manages with our sense of humour.

The scenery takes on a light brown complexion as the Tuscany countryside surrounds us from all sides. There is hardly a word spoken between us as the van ventures deeper into the secluded territory. We are all summoned from our light slumber as the van pulls into the Castello Vichiomaggio – a hotel that provided the backdrop for Kenneth Brannagh's cinematic interpretation of Shakespeare's *Much Ado About Nothing*.

As I haven't seen the movie, I rely on Mark to give me some idea of its significance. There is a small pool and garden maze that intrigues

Mark's six year-old daughter Holly, but I am more interested in the ripe 'ready to pick' peaches on the front lawn.

'I must watch the video when I get back' I tell Mark.

'You won't like it.'

'I'll let you know that I am a big fan of Shakespeare!' declareth I.

'But Keanu Reeves is in it!' he retorts.

'Oh. I hate it already.'

There is a compulsory food stop at a local supermarket where Steve buys pita bread, Cam purchases ham sandwiches while I haul out a 3 kilogram watermelon the size of a beachball. After a couple of bites I am sick of it. Mark wonders whether Holly is really the youngest here.

We poke our heads into San Gimignano – a medieval collection of towers which have stood since the early centuries. And from this point, we get a full 360 degree view of the whole of Tuscany. The vineyards to the East signal our next port of call . . . the Tenuta Torciano Winery. Pier Luigi is the latest in 12 generations of Torcianos who have worked the land to its present state, and have brewed the finest chianti since 1720. He has a firm handshake and a welcoming smile.

He takes me through the vineyards and displays plenty of emotion when it comes to speaking of his wine. The success is in the hard work, the weather, the toil and, most importantly, the love. The Tuscany soil is rough and challenging which must add a degree of difficulty to the process.

He insists that we taste some of his fine collection, providing mineral water and truffle paste with crackers to complete the feast. Fabrizio and Marie Theresa have joined us, so the wine-tasting lasts until every bottle is drunk dry.

There is an athletics track next to the hotel, but I am informed that it is for members of the Athletic Federation only. The rejection doesn't concern me greatly – the fact that I haven't partaken in any physical exercise in nearly two weeks does – so I am tinged with extra guilt as I demolish any plate of greasy bacon sandwiches. The full Italian buffet breakfast will be my undoing.

The local markets operate this morning, with an array of clothing, shoes, sunglasses, materials and make up to choose from. Nothing interests me more than 'people-watching' in these situations, so I sit upon an old brass statue and observe the market ambience. Later in the morning I target a nearby dress stall:

'Hello.'

'Ciao,' mumbles the female owner.

'Parle englais?'

'No!' she snaps, with 'you've just killed my cat' intensity.

'OK, well I would like to buy one of your dresses!'

'No!'

'But I will pay good money.'

'No!'

I hope she goes bankrupt soon. Grumpy thing.

We are now sick of pizza and garlic bread, so when Mark declares that lunch will be taken at 'Senor Buffo's' – a wild boar pasta specialist – we all want to marry him. Buffo is your archetypal Italian chef. Loud, fat, emotional, with big chubby fingers and a king size moustache. He speaks no English but makes it abundantly clear that he is passionate about his food, as he serves monstrous portions of wild boar pasta and iceberg salad. For the first time in ages we eat sensibly without rushing, and the relaxed environment allows wine to be consumed at a leisurely pace.

The return to Siena coincides with a ferocious thunderstorm that soaks the clay dirt paddocks and darkens the sky. Fork lightning dances on the horizon while Fabrizio vigilantly guides us through the torrent.

The Siena Campo is the square in which the Palio was raced in the weekend but since then it has transformed itself into its former glory. The dirt raceway and crowd barriers have been taken down and the undulating surface is now a meeting place for scores of tourists. Four days earlier, this was the battleground of Italy's finest horsemen. I lie on the red brick floor and make eyes at a nearby group of female tourists. I have my sunglasses on and they probably think I'm blind.

Earlier in the week, Marie Theresa had advised us not to bother with the nightclubs. At this time of year, the city's youth migrate to the coast and the clubs are left empty due to their absence. Instead, Italy's biggest rock sensation since . . . er . . . Italy's last rock sensation . . . are playing down at the local amphitheatre and we have tickets. In the end, the need for tickets wasn't necessary as the crowd filters in and out of the half-full concert.

The band are very entertaining, with a style caught between Oasis and Rolling Stones, and the evening rocks into oblivion.

This morning is spent checking out of the Jolly Hotel, and arguing over a 100,000 lira hotel bill for room service extras. A bill I refuse to pay, considering I didn't order any room service. With rock band Negrita still ringing in my ears from last night, I make the situation worse by playing their album in the van stereo.

'At least it's not bloody Coolio!' screams Cam. One person happy at least.

Fields of gold: Nick and Lynette amidst the sunflowers.

An unscheduled stop this morning as Lynette spots a field of fully bloomed sunflowers, and we dive into the thick foliage to capture the moment. The sea of yellow petals is highlighted against the arid expanse of farmland. Steve is in 'cameraman heaven' as he rolls tape over the spectacular scene.

The Hotel De La Ville is the final destination for the week, and we bid farewell to Marie Theresa and then wander into the Plaza to mingle with the locals. There is no room to move this afternoon, as the crowds swarm into the city centre to enjoy the freedom of the city. We complete the shoot by filming a farewell in front of the Duomo which runs along these lines:

'So, thanks for joining us for another episode of Destination Planet Earth,' I start.

'Well, I've had a great time,' Lynette continues.

'From Lynette and myself, it's arrivederci!'

'Ciao!'

'Ciao, bella.'

'Bonsoir?'

Lynette's final farewell (in French) has us rolling on the ground with laughter.

Yet again, Mark has directed a fine show, and we celebrate an entertaining week with a slap-up meal at 'La Bussola Pizza Restaurant' on Porta Rossa Road. There is singing coming from outside the restaurant doors, but we decline the invitation to join the revelry as the pakehas in our group can't sing.

Our focus now turns to packing our bags for trip to the Netherlands.

Apart from the usual cleaning and packing, we also need to make sure all the tapes are stored and correctly labelled. I pay my hotel bill, which ends up significantly more expensive than I ever imagined. I pay for all those fruit salads and fries.

We have arranged to leave at 5.30am, but I am the only one waiting in the foyer this morning. It is rare for the boys to sleep through their alarm calls but a night on the 'bevvies' can deepen slumber. Fabrizio waits patiently as two weary-eyed crew members drag themselves and seventeen pieces of luggage to the departure counter of Meridiana Airways.

The clay-brown fields of Tuscany disappear into a haze of morning sun and heavy cloud cover. I flick through the latest issue of 'FHM' magazine, but turn to notice that the boys can only manage the inside of their eyelids for reading material. The flight is two hours long so, following a quick sandwich, I also fall slowly to sleep – Oasis pumping slowly out of my Walkman.

With only 20 minutes to go, I suddenly feel light-headed. The heat in the cabin has risen drastically, and my head starts to spin. Suddenly, the world turns black and Cam is slapping me on the face. The tears stream down my face, and I immediately assume that I have fainted. Cam calls a hostess for a drink and he cradles my head on his shoulders to prevent me from losing consciousness again. The plane lands and I tentatively walk towards the baggage claim. Cam tells me that he saw me keel over and noticed my eyes had rolled back, and quickly revived me. I am grateful that I was sitting next to him, otherwise I may have widdled my pants on some innocent Italian.

I still feel weak as we leave the airport under the care of Bernie Dunn, our Amsterdam guide and driver. Nigel is waiting at the hotel with his wife Diane and daughter Amy, but Bernie does us the honour of booking the crew into rooms. We all feel shattered so an early night beckons.

Chapter 9 | HOLLAND

Day 56, Saturday 23rd August

The temperature in my room has rocketed to over 30°C and I struggle to breathe, let alone get a decent night's sleep. Even with the windows open and air conditioning set to 'Arctic', the humidity is frighteningly high, so I jump into a cold shower and then meet Nigel for breakfast. The morning free gives me the opportunity to get a haircut and stock up on provisions.

Bernie Dunn is almost as mad as we are, which gives us good reason to interview him on camera. We complement this notion with a trip down the intricate canal system on a riverboat. Bernie left his native America and settled here in 1976 after falling 'victim' to the country's liberal stance on drugs and sex.

He feels there is a genuine spirit to Amsterdam, with the police playing a secondary role to the public's astute awareness and protection of their city ethos. This is reflected in the crime rate – one of the lowest in the Europe, while teenage pregnancies hardly even register. The city also heralds the title 'gay capital of the northern hemisphere', with gay couples openly expressing their feelings in the street with no real fear of recrimination.

Right out of the blue, Bernie whisks a harmonica from his pocket and starts to jam. Yesterday I was basking in Italian sun, now I'm singing *Stand by Me* on a Dutch canal.

Later that afternoon Nigel insists on filming a travel tip about dog pooh. The city has an estimated 50,000 dogs that produce approximately 10,000 kilograms of doodoo every day. Unlike the pollution paranoia in New Zealand they are not expected to scoop the poop, and the city is littered with these 'hazards'. The concept is all rather hysterical, as we skilfully go in search for the biggest 'mound' to film.

'Excuse me madam, but have you seen a big pile of turd near here recently?'

'Pardon me, officer. Can you point me in the direction of the nearest pooh please.'

Although the scene causes much hilarity, there is genuine recognition among us that the problem is rather serious. Many dog owners allow their animals to soil in the canal which has heightened public concern for the hygiene and health of the environment.

Along with the liberal attitude to 'homosexuality' in this town, there is a popular and lively gay entertainment culture to go with it. The 't'Sluije' restaurant is our first stop on the night life agenda and, while Mary has a boogie behind the bar, I talk to two of the restaurant performers, Catya and Lulu, in their dressing room. They are both transvestites who perform various vocal numbers while balancing on perilously awkward high heel shoes and equally extravagant dresses. These acts include *Don't Cry For Me Argentina* and *Wind Beneath My Wings*, the last of which brings the house down.

'Are you coming to the Big Party?' asks Lulu (real name probably Bruce) as we depart.

'What Big Party?' we ask.

'Oh, only the biggest party of the year in the whole of Europe!'

'We haven't got tickets.'

'Don't worry. Just mention that you're a camera crew and you'll be treated like *queens*.'

Er, yes.

Her suggestion seems to be the best option, so our footsteps lead us to 'Club It' where the 'Hollywood Party' is already starting to attract a crowd. The Big Party isn't big at all, it's HUGE! The screaming masses flood out into the streets, where numerous transvestite icons arrive in limousines Oscar-style. It is the biggest collection of freaks, trannies and gays that we will ever see and, although the surreal scene would be daunting to any conservative being, the carnival atmosphere generated is unbelievable.

Being the only film crew attracts plenty of attention, and I get the opportunity to interview plenty of talent, while others invite themselves to the lens. I get propositioned by one monster in high heels:

'Ooo, hello love. How long are YOU in town for?'

'Um, I have to go. Sorry.'

She has bigger thighs than Olo Brown. I run away very fast.

We discover, as the crew enter the club, that we have only dipped our toes in the pond of weirdness – the club is also hosting the 'Hollywood Party Beauty Pageant' and a whole array of acts strut across an enormous stage. The evening is brilliantly coordinated, and the dancing continues into the early hours. Mary has just arrived from a nightmarish flight from Auckland, struggled with sleep, is suffering from jet lag and is now surrounded by the biggest freak show in history. She absorbs it all. Good work, girl.

Reception has supplied me with a fan that, set to full rotation, manages to drop the temperature slightly and I achieve a comfortable sleep. *Shortland Street's* Mary Lose has been struggling to put more than two hours of slumber together, so we are relieved when Nigel delays kick-off until 1.30pm. Attempt to go for a run, but last no more than 10 minutes in the heat. I have yet to see the sun in Amsterdam, the clouds providing a humidity blanket that is the main cause of unease.

We have decided to conduct a 'covert' operation in the Red Light district as Nigel would like some walking shots of myself and Mary surveying the area. Due to the ban on cameras in the district, we need to set up a concealed pencil camera and battery pack that Steve will operate while it remains hidden on his person. The camera is only the size of a large cigar and is positioned in his underarm, while the cords are run inside his shirt into the battery pack on his back. I'm not entirely convinced that it won't be detected, and even though we run through various scenarios and methods of concealment, there is no safety guarantee on this one.

Steve is comfortable with his new toy, and we arrange to drive into the outskirts of the Red Light, disembark and walk through with minimal fuss. Mary and I are to keep a distance from the camera with Nigel, Bernie and Cam acting as lookouts. Sadly our pre-arranged plans fall flat, as we are unavoidably separated a few metres from the van when we arrive. Mary, Nigel and I decide to wait on a nearby bridge for the other party to return. It will only be a matter of minutes before they notice our absence.

Ten minutes turns into twenty. And then to thirty.

At this stage we begin to get a little concerned, and can only assume the boys have gotten lost in the labyrinth of canal bridges and alleys. Our anxiety is relieved temporarily when the familiar silhouettes of Bernie and

The crew ouside Amsteredans Rijksmuseum. Left to right: Steve Orsbourn, Nigel Carpenter, Cam McGrath.

Steve appear around the corner. However it is immediately obvious that two things are missing:

The soundman. And the camera.

Nigel goes quite pale when Steve instructs us to leave the area promptly. Only when we are in the safe confines of the Hertz rental van, leaving the Red Light area hastily on our return to the hotel, does Steve manage to explain the incident. Realising that the group had become separated, they decided to continue deeper into the district with Bernie and Cam keeping a weary eye on the surroundings.

Steve believed he had captured some fantastic footage and even had the nerve to approach and converse with some of the prostitutes, while keeping the camera rolling. Unfortunately one of the girls spotted the lens underneath Steve's clothing and made a grab for it, at the same time alerting several bouncers in the alley.

Within seconds, Steve was set upon by a number of large men who were making frantic attempts to snatch the camera from him. In a superb piece of quick thinking, Cam, who was ten metres behind, rushed in to help by wrestling the gear out of Steve's grasp and racing off into the depths of the night.

Only one bouncer pursued, while the rest manhandled Steve into a safehouse and demanded the tape so it could be destroyed. Proclaiming his innocence, and having no obvious incriminating evidence, he threw them his wallet and escaped through a side door. All within the space of a few seconds.

Nigel's jaw had dropped to his ankles as Steve was telling his story and I was still half-expecting him to start laughing uncontrollably and reveal the joke. Sadly, it never did and we were now faced with a serious situation – and two major questions. Where was the camera gear? But, more importantly, did Cameron make a clean getaway? We returned to The Estheria, dropped off Steve, and returned to the scene of the crime. Nigel and I surveyed for about an hour before discovering that Cam had turned up safe and sound at the hotel. With camera gear. You would've heard Nigel's sigh of relief from Norway.

That night's viewing of footage was the best yet, as we discovered that the camera had continued to roll as the ruckus erupted. We all got to view the action at close hand, plenty of scuffling feet and muffled shouts but what tension!

'What an operation!' screams Cam.

'That is a classic DPE moment.'

'TV3 were on standby just in case there was real trouble.'

'We had Bernie! There's no problem when Bernie's around.'

Back in my room, my adventures with the fan continue. I have positioned it almost 2 inches away from my face, as the heat in the room becomes increasingly unbearable. A huge breakfast gives me some reward, but the humming of the fan still rings in my ear.

Bernie has a vast collection of tapes in the van but I prefer to torture him with my hip hop mixes. He doesn't disapprove, he just doesn't listen. There seems to be an endless supply of drinks emerging from Bernie's chilly bin, diet cokes and mineral water aplenty, which means we re-hydrate on the move.

They don't allow fluids in the Rijksmuseum however, but they have a fairly good reason – it's full of Rembrandts. The collection is so vast that the marketing representative predicts two days are needed to cover each exhibit properly.

The most famous piece on show is Rembrandt's 'The Night Watch'. Painted in 1642 it is in fact a misnomer, as it portrays a day scene but only those subjects who paid money got featured in the light. The rest being submerged into a dark background.

Back in the van Bernie slips on 'The Beatles Greatest Hits', as we pull out of the Rijks car park, which hints at irony given that our next stop is the Amsterdam Hilton. No-one needs reminding of those historic lyrics:

'Christ, you know it ain't easy, you know how hard it can be,
The way things are going, they're goin' to crucify me.

Paris to the Amsterdam Hilton, talking in our beds for a week,
The newspapers said, say what're you doing in bed,
I said we're only trying to get us some peace.'

John Lennon has no hope of 'resting in peace' with this crew around. Dressed in wigs and glasses, Mary and I flaunt it on the double bed in Suite 1901, the same one used back in March of 1969 for the famous Bed-In for Peace. Shortly before midnight on March 24th twenty-eight years ago, John Lennon and Yoko Ono removed all the furniture and lay in bed for a week. Mary and I want to do the same, but only because we're too tired to move.

This famous room provokes varying emotions within the crew. Bernie is re-living his hippy days by dancing wildly around the room, Nigel flicks through the hotel brochure on the sofa while Steve plays a number of Beatle CD's on the suite stereo system. Cam shares similar feelings to me – a feeling similar to that of wanting to scream in an empty church, or farting loudly in an examination room – so we initiate a mass brawl among the duvets and pillows. It proves to be so hysterical that we set the camera rolling.

We sign 'Destination Planet Earth' in the visitor book, pinch a bottle of champagne from the mini-bar and leave. If you're keen on sleeping with the spirit of John and Yoko, ring the Hilton. It'll only cost you a couple of thousand dollars.

The last stop is the city Sex Museum, or the 'Venus Temple', which sits opposite the Railway station. Upon entering you are exposed to the largest collection of playing cards, Victorian viewing machines, sketches, old porno crockery, magazines, paintings and ancient photographs depicting sex that you will could stumble on (apart from under your younger brother's bed). The history of sexual positions is covered in one section, while I make a hasty retreat to the sexual acts exhibition which features photo explanations of every conceivable kind of sex performed.

'I'm sure I saw a donkey in one of them' I report back to the lads.

'Oh, that's sick' laughs Cam, as he eyeballs a pair of Victorian wooden breasts.

I am surprised at the number of older people that are wandering through each exhibition. It is a shrine for the 'randy student' or 'giggling teenager' types but hardly a Sunday stroll for the older generations. They don't seem to be too disgusted as I notice each couple spending lengthy spells at the retractable penis statue or Marilyn Monroe's flying knickers. Good on them. The liberal atmosphere of Amsterdam seems to affect everyone. (Or perhaps that should be infect.)

I watch the Dutch channel this morning, trying desperately to understand what they are saying. After an hour I have discovered that 'ja' means 'yes'. We have another free morning so Mary and I sit and chat over an orange juice while soaking up the Holland sunshine. The kitchen staff sit patiently, waiting for us to leave. Which we do. Three hours later.

Amsterdam has such a complex network of canals that I insist on keeping a map in my wallet for fear of getting lost within the labyrinth of the central city. A sandwich and mineral water is my only purchase as I then return to my room and grab an hour of sleep.

Our faithful driver is patiently waiting on time. Bernie is growing to become one of the gang. His singing, however, is appalling and we constantly remind him that Paul McCartney sang in tune – unlike Bernie's squealing rendition of *Love Me Do*. His friendly and optimistic approach is an extra boost to the crew, as we pile into the van at 6.00pm to shoot some city action.

Quite by chance the city university is in the throes of 'Orientation Week', prompting a tidal wave of young people into the popular bars around town. One such haunt, Mister Coco's, is flushed out by at least 200 blond-haired Dutch women and Cam is nearly ill with the overload. It is quite a sight. (For purposes of censorship, the reminder of the night's activities will not be recorded. This is due to the diary notes being either misplaced or lost. On purpose)

The sun is desperately trying to squeeze its head through the cloud band this morning. The couple in the room across the corridor were arguing so loudly they woke me at 6.00am:

'Where is my shirt? I don't know where you keep putting my shirt!'

'Shuddap Laurie, for goodness sake. It's in the wardrobe.'

'Hmm. Goodness me. It's such a chore, isn't it!' blah, blah, blah.

If it isn't the blistering heat in my room, then it's Laurie's shirts next door.

Budget Rentals have given us a VW Golf Cabriolet to play with this morning, which we drive into the countryside. It's only 20 minutes away on the motorway, but the contrast couldn't be more extreme. The sight of cramped high-rise apartments diffuses into a flat, misty grassland. The grass dew glistens in the sunlight, but on closer inspection I notice it is due to a high level of surface water from the dike outlets. Bernie reveals that the whole surrounding area of countryside is below sea level and the balance of water is indeed sensitive but controlled.

SHORTLAND STREET's Mary Lose and Nick go Dutch at the Katwouder Molen.

We enter Broek in Waterland, the area that was reclaimed in the 16th century from fifteen lakes. They drain the lake 24 hours a day into the canals to keep the land dry for grazing, and Bernie tells us that Napoleon and Czar Peter the Great were frequent visitors to this area. Cam is feeling peckish which, appropriately, leads us to Jacob Hoeve's Edam Cheese Factory. I take the opportunity to dress up in traditional Dutch woman's clothing, prompting our host, Hans, to ask:

'So, Nick. You do this sort of thing everywhere you visit? Dressing in woman's clothing?' A quizzical look appearing on his face.

I reply with firm assurance. 'Oh no. No, no, no, no, no . . . well, yes.'

We all jump at the chance for free nibbles, and start tasting various strains of Edam cheese – from smoky to bacon to goat's milk – and even experience some genuine farm action in the goat stables. Due to the large number of tourists, the goats are friendly enough to touch and play with.

A canal, a boat, and a VW Golf convertible, Monnikendamm.

In typical goat-nibbling tradition they attempt to chew through the camera cables, Cam's sound boom and my trousers.

As we travel north to Katwouder, I cast my mind back to a postcard I received from a friend in primary school who lived in Rotterdam. It featured a 'typical' landscape littered with windmills but, as I have noticed on occasions when poking my head out of the van window, I am casting my eyes over a largely 'windmill-less' countryside. Bernie explains that it is due to the efficient nature of the mechanical water control – therefore there's no real need for wind power. Just as my hopes sink, the Katwouder Molen windmill appears on the horizon in all its glory.

Raoul Boulangier is the 'windmill keeper' and proudly proclaims that his 'girl' (called Bridget) pumps up to 60,000 litres a minute to keep the nearby land from being flooded.

Raoul is saddened by the fact that there used to be around ten thousand windmills in the Netherlands before the steam pump was introduced in the 1850's. Bridget is an oldie but goldie – as proven in 1988 when the electric pump broke and wind power was called in as a valuable (and more reliable) substitute!

The countryside is not dramatic but the cool breeze and fresh air is a kind alternative to choking fumes, and we cruise through the nearby villages of Edam, Monnikendamm and Zouder Wouder before heading back into the city. Nigel insists on travelling back in the topless VW, which he soon regrets as the skies open and the torrential rain soaks the occupants. I laugh from the safety of the warm minibus.

On our return, we pass a drunken gentleman in the high street having a wee and exposing himself in the middle of the street. He seems to be totally undeterred by the fact he is causing a traffic jam and grins proudly at the passing vehicles. As fate would have it, we pull up directly opposite this rather obscene performance to which we all applaud loudly out the window. Smug smiles of adulation turn quickly to horror as the 'unmasked crusader' turns his attention to washing the exterior of our van by 'natural means'. Bernie runs a red light in his haste to escape.

That night is spent watching the day's footage, which seems to have become a daily ritual. Room 411 is centre-stage and Bernie usually provides the drinks. He has become an honorary crew member, and says he will find it hard to come across another group of 'fun loving criminals' like ourselves.

It's our last day of filming, and it starts with Mary looking through the Van Gogh Museum. There are four floors of exhibits containing more than 200 paintings and 580 drawings by the Dutch master, originally part of his brother's collection. Van Gogh died at the age of only 37 years and his extensive works came from an inspired period of just ten years. His final years of life were full of personal torture. In a fit of delusion, induced by a rare form of epilepsy, he cut off his ear lobe, and then died by a self-inflicted gun wound to the chest. His work is dark and disturbing but brilliant.

Like most of the art centres we visit, the authorities allow us to film the interior before the galleries are open to the public. This is done to avoid inconvenience to public and cameraman alike!

One of the gallery attendants is a huge Surinamese woman called Saskia, who has the voice of Darth Vader but a sweet smile. She pokes fun at us by pretending not to know of New Zealand's whereabouts:

'Oh, you must be from that island off Australia, no? Or is it in Holland?'

Funnily enough she is right on both accounts. While we consider ourselves to be more than an island off Oz, there is a territory called Zeeland in Holland from which our name was determined. She is more knowledgeable than we give her credit for.

I have seen nearly every major gallery in the world by now so, without sounding too blasé, I sit back (ignoring the wealth of art at my disposal) and scribble this diary amidst the masterpieces.

Nigel is well known for throwing surprises at the film crew, but nothing has prepared me for our next stop – Gary Christmas' Backstage Café. Bernie has told me that this is a hugely popular haunt for the city's 'extreme' personalities.

Gary Christmas is the owner and proves to be as entertaining and colourful as I imagined. He and his twin brother Greg were born in Boston to mother Mary, (Yep, Mary Christmas!) and forged careers as cabaret singers which sent them to all corners of the earth. He has lived in Amsterdam for 18 years and set up the Backstage Café. There are plenty of brightly coloured oddities like pink cardigans and fluorescent bobble hats that adorn the shop, as well as a humorous menu of sandwiches labelled with such delights as 'Big Bazookas' and 'Wobbly Bum'. Gary gives us plenty of advice for good nightclubs and some interesting theories on the Red Light District.

I get to try on some of his extravagant clothes including white clogs and kaleidoscope pants. I look in the mirror and shake my head in disbelief. Nigel and the boys are laughing. Loudly.

I sleep deeply and wake with enough dirt in my eye to start a garden. Another day, another airport. Paranoid that I will faint again, I make a special effort to stock up body fluids to ensure proper hydration. Unfortunately this prompts several visits to the toilet and eventually I get sick of drinking mineral water so settle for a dry sandwich.

Edinburgh becomes a small blip on the monitor as we soar to 15,000 feet on British Airways Flight X180 and by 10.00am we land at East Midlands airport. I inform Cam and Steve that I went to university only a few miles away and wondered if we could see if we went up to the observation deck. Cam replies with equal gusto: 'You're an idiot'.

We have been on the road far too long.

It's hard to understand why we need to travel via East Midlands and Glasgow to get to Edinburgh but it seems that nothing is easy when it comes to international travel. Landing in Glasgow provides a raw introduction to the British autumn as the chilly wind attacks the lightly clothed crew. Johanna Campbell is our Tourist Board rep for this week and she creates a cheerful atmosphere by playing The Proclaimers in the car cassette player as soon as we hit the motorway south:

'Well, I would walk 500 miles, and I would walk 500 more
Just to be the man who walked 500 miles to fall down at yer door'

We collect Anita McNaught (this week's co-presenter) and head to Edinburgh. She has been working for BBC World and is pleased to be out of the studio environment. Our director assures her that she will be as far from civilisation as humanly possible this week.

Mark gives us the afternoon off, so I meet up with an old university friend who lives nearby. A massive feed of pizza and garlic bread washed down with fruit juice and memories of rebellious student days perform an ideal battery-recharge. I am starting to feel the effects of nearly four weeks on the road, but this is the first chance I've had to break away from the rest of the crew.

We all meet again in town and visit the Iguana nightspot for a quick drink. The night is young but there is a real buzz as the Edinburgh Festival grinds to halt tonight with several final performances by leading acts. One of the most popular acts this season has been 'Mika' – a cabaret act from home – and we get front row seats to the command perform-ance. It is a mix of re-vamped songs with funky choreographed routines, and powerful verse from all three Maori performers. It is great to see them doing so well, and they deservedly strike a popular cord with the audience.

By midnight, it is time to go home. The only available accom-modation during this busy Festival period is 25 minutes from the centre of town in a suburban bed and breakfast, but I'm asleep before we get there.

CHAPTER 10 | **DEATH OF A PRINCESS**

Day 63, Saturday 30th August

The call is midday and, due to a crisp blue sky, I go for a light run in a nearby park. I am now feeling the effects of spending five weeks on the road, and seem to be running on automatic as I plod over the grassy field. My walkman refuses to work properly and, in a fit of frustration, I attempt to fix the faulty operation by kicking it forcefully into the air. End of walkman. I sulk all the way back to the hotel.

'What's with the sad face?'

'I broke my Walkman.'

'On what?'

'My foot. I kicked it.'

'You're an idiot.'

Over the last five years I have vacationed in Scotland on at least ten different occasions, and have enjoyed each visit immensely. The weather has always been exceptional and the trend continues today as the bright sun shines down. We are staying at Ashcroft Bed and Breakfast, hosted by a delightful family, in the suburb of East Calder – a sleepy hollow that has a post office and about thirty pubs. I amble into a sandwich shop and grab a quick bite to eat.

Johanna, looking a little worse for wear, collects us at midday and by one o'clock we are all strolling down the Royal Mile in the crisp sunshine. The many street performers that camped down on the tiles for the last month have left, but a vigilant few remain. One coloured African man contorts his body into various shapes, while a London tramp makes peas disappear up his nose. Anita and I talk with locals, and a student minstrel gives me a blow on his bagpipes. I blow too hard and burst one of his flute connections.

I stop an elderly lady in a green soccer shirt and ask her where she's going:

'Why, the biggest game of the year, laddie,' she drawls. 'Ye should go!'

She supports Hibernian, an Edinburgh team who are facing local derby opposition in Hibernians down the road at Easter Road Stadium. I ask whether we would have the opportunity to get tickets:

'Ooo, e down't know boy. E'vry man and 'is doog will be there!' she says.

'Who should we cheer for when we get there?'

'HIBS!' Her scream almost knocks me over.

Mark, who loves his soccer, promptly abandons the day's filming and we head off to Easter Road. Sadly 15,600 people were quicker than us to purchase tickets. The gates are closed before we have a chance to get a look in. We concede defeat and listen outside the stadium to the roar that indicates Hibernian have scored. Steve has never seen a British soccer match, and after hearing Mark and myself talk of fond memories from previous experiences, it is disappointing to have come so close.

Several circuits of the stadium in the hope of a stray ticket prove fruitless, so with heavy hearts we plod off.

All is not lost, as Mark, Steve and myself climb Charlton Hill for a view of the Old Town and Edinburgh Castle, and take a few photos on the Greek Monument – built in memory of those who died in the Napoleonic Wars by the people of Edinburgh. Craving food, we stumble into a rugby memorabilia pub, and end up sitting underneath what looks like a genuine All Black match jersey:

'It's got Number 10 on the back.'

'I wonder if it's Foxy's.'

'You're right lad,' the landlord shouts. 'That is the jersey of Grant Fox. The only time he has ever played in the white jersey, and he gave it to us!'

We raise our glasses to Scotland, Celtic and Foxy.

Sunday, August 31st 1997 was one of those days that will always be remembered. The morning was quiet and still as I wrestled myself from a deep sleep. Naturally I flick on the television to watch the BBC's morning show and settle down between the sheets. In a semi-conscious state, I am aware of a startling news flash coming from the TV speaker:

'. . . and it is believed that the paparazzi photographers were pursuing the car at the time. French medical teams have now left the site of the crash, and the police have escorted a number of press representatives away for questioning. It is believed that Prince Charles is comforting the young princes at this very moment.'

Startled, I jump upright in my bed.

The whole world has woken to the news that Diana, Princess of Wales, has been killed in a car accident in Paris and there is no worse place that the news is received than in Great Britain. The repeated images of Diana's mangled car flicker over all four television channels this morning and there is an obvious sombre mood as we all file in for breakfast at Ashcroft dining room.

'The Princess of Wales is dead' the news break echoes from the lips of every newsreader from the BBC through to Channel 5. 'Diana. Rest in peace'.

My immediate concern is that the Royal Palaces, that we were due to visit, will be closed and an anticipated day of mourning may interrupt our shooting schedule. Mark is anticipating a move to London to cover the story, on the instruction of TV3. The call never comes and we are on the road by 10.00am.

It is difficult to strike up conversation as the radio coverage is dominated by the various analysis of the accident. Anita is absorbing as much as possible, while Cam is becoming annoyed with all the opinions. I tend to agree with him, and can only marvel at the numerous theories and scandals that will emerge from this most bizarre occasion.

'This is going to be bigger than JFK,' Johanna pipes.

'It'll be a case of where were you when Di was killed.'

Somewhat ironically, the weather has turned sour and even though we are able to shoot the Firth of Forth railway bridge and the birthplace of Robert Louis Stevenson, its impending demise prevents any more action and we abandon the day's shooting.

The journey to Rathcluthan Guest House takes a half an hour, and I rejoice at the sound of a warm shower running. There is a sneaking suspicion within the crew that our services may yet be required in London but, until it happens, we won't lose sleep over it. TV3 will need to get in contact with the crew in the next 12 hours if any coverage is required.

The inevitable phone call arrives at about 2.00am and I am woken by Mark and Steve banging on the door.

'Wake up boy!'

'What's the matter?'

'We're going to London!'

'What's the time?'

'Two o'clock.'

'When is our plane leaving?'

'Six.'

TV3 have decided to fly us to London this morning to cover any leading stories that may break in the days leading to the funeral. None of us are surprised by the decision but it is puzzling that it has taken 24 hours before notification was received. We all concede that it's out of our control, and Edinburgh Airport has 5 extra punters in the early hours.

Not surprisingly, the city of London is caught up in a state of sombre reflection, although wandering through its busy streets, I fail to see any real tangible sign of the sorrow. As the headline in a daily tabloid states: 'Life goes on in London'.

We have been booked into the Hospitality Inn on Bayswater, only a stone's throw from Kensington Palace, and we all crash into bed for a few hours of sleep before heading into town to film some of the emotional scenes at Buckingham Palace. While the team film some various snippets I head out to Kensington Palace to sit among the scores of mourners and bouquets of flowers. Although there is obvious sorrow, there seems to exist a remarkable sense of 'union' between the people gathered there. Black, white, Asian, gay, all walks of life united in grief. These are the images that I see on the television that night and I feel privileged to have been a part of it.

Earlier that afternoon I had bumped into an old schoolfriend near Piccadilly Circus and had talked about the effect that it had on New Zealanders. He was genuinely shocked, and couldn't believe he was in the middle of London when it happened.

'You can't get closer than this, can ya?'

As macabre as it sounded, I had to agree.

'I was in New Zealand last week, and now I'm closer than I'll ever be to the Royals,' he smiled. 'My mum is so upset. She wants me to go to the funeral.'

'I should too. But we could be well on our way to Scotland again'

With 8 million people expected to come into the city for the funeral, I can't help thinking that the best view would be in front of the telly. That night I lent on my window sill and looked over the city that I had grown to know so well over the years. For once, it seemed silent.

The boys and Anita were out filming until the early hours and Mark returns looking like death. In situations like this, everyone needs to pull together but our director is feeling the most pressure. It seems bizarre that 24 hours ago we were wallowing in the pleasant backdrop of Scotland and are now neck-deep in one of modern time's most significant world events.

Yesterday, I was getting annoyed at the almost sycophantic outpouring of grief. However, being so closely involved I am aware of the natural affection that the nation had for their Princess. I switch through all of the TV channels – out of respect the schedules have been toned down – the radio stations are all playing sombre, classical music, and the newspapers are all dominated by full page, colour spreads. All sports fixtures have been cancelled this weekend, the first time in British history.

The Diana saga continues as the tabloids are now pointing the finger at the limo driver. Look like everybody will be put under the microscope including the Royal Family. No word from home yet regarding our near future, although several scenarios have been toyed with. The Scotland shoot could well be abandoned, or delayed until after the funeral – which has now been confirmed for Saturday.

Either way, I am not required until that news comes through so I have a relatively easy ride. I help Steve and Cam with the gear but this proves to be pointless as most of the shooting takes place in the early hours (to keep with NZ time) and I am fast asleep. The boys are working overtime and Anita is beside herself with stress. The whole idea of journalism sucks to me and I don't envy her position.

It is remarkably convenient that she was available during this time, and that Mark Everton had directed news before. TV3 have saved the cost of a plane trip for some home-based crew, and prevented a time delay in getting someone over. Apparently Paul Holmes is here already. Suddenly the whole idea of shooting a travel show seems worthless and worryingly insignificant. The future of the shoot lies in the hands of higher authorities so, for me, it is now a waiting game.

Jim Bolger appears on the television, sending the nation's condolences. I phone my parents in New Zealand to pass on the recent developments and then drift off to sleep.

Dawn brings with it the first full day I have had off since arriving in Europe. It gives me the opportunity to jump on the tube and seek out old haunts but I simply browse around record shops and pop in to see the Robert Carlisle film *The Full Monty*. Much to my surprise, the national anthem is played before the main feature as a sign of respect. Nearly all sports fixtures have been postponed in the weekend and no shops will be open, it sounds to me as if London will be best and worst place to be on Saturday.

News at last! A phone call confirms that the Scotland shoot will resume tomorrow, although Anita will stay behind to cover the funeral. The BBC are rumoured to have up to 100 cameras set up to follow the procession and return of the body to the Northampton estate, so one TV3 camera won't make much of a difference.

The news is well received as we were dreading the thought of staying for any longer. Steve and Cam manage a few hours of sleep while Mark is busy editing for *Newsnight*. He hasn't had any sleep for 30 hours and is looking exhausted. He will be working throughout the night, and will have to run on nervous energy to get through. That and plenty of Coke – the kind you drink.

On Thursday the 'Destination Planet Earth' train is rolling again. We arrive at the airport expecting to leave at 9.00am but discover there is no such flight. The 10.00am is our only option and we sit in Burger King listening to Steve's fascinating story of how he had to punch a policeman last night. Apparently he was in the way of the camera.

By 2.00pm that afternoon I am strolling up to the 18th hole at St. Andrew's Golf Course, pretending to acknowledge an imaginary crowd cheering me on. Looking over the magnificent (albeit windswept) course, it's easy to understand why they decide to hold the British Open here. The scenery is pleasant but not too intense, and the greens are impeccably kept.

You need a 15 or less handicap to be able to play, plus a bucket full of money, and it attracts mainly American tourists who try to follow in the footsteps of Colin Montgomery, Ian Woosnam and the like.

I notice a 'No Women' sign outside one of the conference rooms and poke fun at Johanna:

'Looks like you won't be going in there then?'

'I wouldn't want to!' she barks.

Neither would I, to be honest. Stuffy and pompous.

The St. Andrew's course runs parallel to the beach front – the site of an equally famous sporting pursuit. It was on this area of coastline that the closing scene of *Chariots of Fire* was filmed, and Vangelis tinkled the ivories for that memorable soundtrack.

The lads film me running up and down the sandy stretch in an attempt to look remotely like an Olympic athlete. Despite the notion that we are still in the depths of the northern hemisphere summer and the sun is toasty enough to call hot, the sea is unbelievably cold and my feet quickly turn numb as I pose for the camera.

Enough of the childish larking about and time for some history!

St. Andrew's Castle has a subtle reminder of Scotland's bloody past. On the road leading up to the entrance, there is a symbol 'GW' engraved into a plague. This symbol marks the spot where, in 1546, the religious reformer George Wishart was burnt at the stake. His execution was ordered by the Cardinal Beaton. Wishart's mates got their revenge on the Cardinal by slitting his throat, hanging his body out the window, and then pickling him in a huge jar of brine. Yum!

The light has rapidly deteriorated and we call it a day.

'How far away is the hotel?' I ask Johanna, noticing that Mark and Cam have already fallen asleep in the car.

'Och, it's only down the road,' she chimes.

Three hours later we arrive at Dutthill Guest House near Carrbridge. In the middle of absolutely nowhere. We managed to break up the trip by stopping to film the Highland scenery and also got the opportunity to win some money off Cam. I spotted some cattle in a nearby field, as Steve was filming, and told Cam that I could serenade the cows to come closer. He doubted me.

Several renditions of *Amazing Grace* were not enough, but as soon as I started bellowing *Flower of Scotland*, the dozy animals crept up to the fence to get a better view.

'See, what did I tell ya?'

'They're only wondering where the hideous noise is coming from.'

'They love it.'

'Why don't you try something they'll like?'

'Okay, *Old MacDonald had a farm. E, I, E, I, O . . . .*'

By the time we arrive at our accommodation it is 11.35pm. Mark refuses to unpack his bags from the car, and simply walks into his room and falls asleep. We all follow suit.

The guest house owners will not let us leave before having a full English breakfast of bacon, eggs and hash browns, so we indulge ourselves. Twice. It gives Mark a chance to plan the rest of the week – something he simply hasn't had time to do. With Anita in London, the focus has changed from a two presenter show, to a one-man presentation. Anita will feature prominently in the Edinburgh segment.

We are feeding reindeer this morning, and meet our guides Tilly and Liz at 9.00am at the entrance of their nature reserve. It's hard to believe that 24 hours earlier we were coughing up car fumes in London Town, and now in the heart of the Highlands breathing cool, fresh oxygen and, well, feeding reindeer!

This is a popular tourist attraction during the summer months, and in their natural habitat the reindeer are tame and friendly. Tilly and Liz coax them down from their higher ground by screaming out a feeding call. I can't spell it so I won't put it in the diary. The beasts thunder over the hill towards the muesli-grain feed and for a moment I am frightened they won't stop, but the girls have complete control and they proceed to stroke and pat their 'babies'.

Nick, Tilly and Liz coax the reindeer down for a bite.

The reindeer are native to Scotland and are impervious to the chilly temperatures that whip around the Highland Plains. Their furry coats and majestic antlers are fantastic to touch, and I get quite close as the creatures gobble muesli from my hand. Tilly has names for each of the 150 reindeer that stalk the reserve and I put her to the test by pointing out random choices:

'What's that one?'

'Frieda.'

'That one?'

'Gemima.'

'And that one?'

'Zeus.'

'What about those two?'

'Bentley and Ross.'

'Any Rudolph?'

'Are you taking the piss?'

I can't believe I asked that question. She has probably heard it a thousand times over the years, but she still manages a quiet laugh for the camera. Steve and Cam put down their gear in order to spend some quality time mingling with the lovable animals.

We drive north to the most famous lake in the world. A lake that could fit the world's population inside its empty hollow three times over. A lake that is over 300 metres deep. And a lake that is home to the most feared monster on the planet. Loch Ness.

The dark waters lap at the loch shore as Dave Horricks unloads his Canadian canoe. Dave owns and operates his own adventure activity company that caters for the 'outdoor' enthusiast, and includes rafting, diving, boating and canoeing in his packages. Today Cam, Mark and I venture out in a large Canadian-style canoe with Dave at the helm. I look over the side into the murky depths and let my imagination run wild. Dave is convinced there is something down there but I think the Tourist Board is paying him to say it.

Loch Ness monsters: McGrath, Orsbourn and Mark Everton search for the elusive beast.

Once dried off, the DPE van sets off again. Mark's socks are soaked, and I am virtually undressed in the back seat – sitting beside the warm breath of the air-conditioner. We have two more stops before we finish, the first being the site of The Battle of Culloden. Thousands of soldiers were killed on this derelict marshland as the victorious army marched towards the Highland clearances. The outcome makes up a significant part of Scottish history – Gaelic was banned, as was wearing tartan, and the clan system abolished, resulting in the destruction of a way of life. It was during this time that the Scots were sent abroad to places like Australia and Dunedin.

The final stop is another historic site in the form of Urquhart Castle which overlooks the Loch. The commanding position of this battlement ensured that whoever ran the Castle, had power over the Highlands. Several photos are taken and then we give Johanna quick directions to

Urquhart Castle.

the nearest pub – which happens to double up as our hotel, The Glenmoriston Arms in Inverness. Tonight is our lucky night as the Scottish Tourist Board offer to pay for our dinner.

I am halfway through my mushroom bake when I hear a breaking news story on the TV, from BBC headquarters in London:

'It has been reported from Calcutta this evening that Mother Theresa has passed away.'

Steve lets out a laugh. Not out of disrespect but disbelief. Two of the most famous icons of modern history dead within the space of a week. This whole shoot is becoming even more bizarre. There is no shortage of conversation at the dinner table tonight. We all dig into a hearty meal of steak and roast potatoes.

Due to the hectic nature of the past week much of the show's content will come from the footage that we shoot today. There is a lingering whiff of mushroom bake between my teeth as I drag myself from my marshmallow duvet in the early hours. Last night some drunken local spun me a tale of how a landslide, bought on by the adverse weather, almost demolished the hotel last week. I had laughed in his face – dismissing his story as a fib. This morning I walk outside and see, with the aid of the morning light, a slip of land banked up against the hotel wall.

It is the morning of Diana's funeral and we are in the most remote wilderness in the whole of the United Kingdom. I have been given the chance to do some trout fishing in a loch so remote that it doesn't have a name. We meet our guide, James, who drives us deeper into the Highland countryside in his rusty Combi van. He is an ex-Marine Academy instructor and has circumnavigated the globe with his work. Nowadays, give him a rod and a loch and the man is in heaven.

He takes daily trips to his hidden Loch for sixty quid a head, and reckons the accessibility and beauty of the Highlands make it popular with outdoor adventurers who like to fish for trout. He assures me there are fish to be caught and after a quick lesson in 'fly casting' I perch myself on a rock and happily cast away. The eerie silence is only broken by Mark's barking orders.

Thirty minutes later there are no bites, and Mark admits defeat. The joy of catching a fish on camera has been denied. I am about to withdraw my rod from the water when a slight tug almost throws me off the bank. Ha! Success! A baby trout – but still a mighty catch.

I am ecstatic: 'I could fill this whole Loch with my ego!'

Back in 1994 I climbed to the top of Ben Nevis (the highest mountain in Britain) but any chance of retracing those steps are washed away in a nasty downfall. When it comes to a choice of shooting the Glen Coe (the underlying valley) in the fierce shower or eating toasted sandwiches in the local . . . well, you guess.

When the weather clears, Johanna burns rubber all the way to Stirling Castle before we lose valuable light, and we visit the place where William Wallace gathered his armies to take on the likes of King Edward's troops. As the song says:

'That wee bit hill and glen that stood against him
Proud Edward's army, and sent him homewards,
tae think again'

The statue of Wallace stands almost 7 foot tall (close to his actual height) but Mel Gibson's likeness – in the souvenir shop – is quite pathetic in comparison. There is a stone bridge in the town centre, called Stirling Bridge, which is the actual place where Wallace waited for the English to cross. As they were halfway there, he attacked and won a famous victory. There are two curious local children watching us film, and I strike up a conversation with them both:

'Are you two from Stirling?' I ponder.

'Aye,' they both say in unison. They are brother and sister, and talk in 'shotgun' Scottish.

'Can you sing *Flower of Scotland* for the camera?'

'Aye, but hoo much are ye ginna pay us?'

'Nothing.'

'Okay then,' he giggles as his sister hides behind him.

I join him in a rather up-tempo rendition of his national anthem, and then pay them a pound for their trouble. They are pleasant, and working class to the core. As we jump in the car, the young fella shouts out:

'Ye say ye from Noo Zealand, ay?'

I nod in reply.

'That Jonah Lomu. He eats lots of pizzas, aye?'

It is dark when we pull into the Apex International Hotel in Edinburgh, and Cam lets out a huge bellow when we unload: 'Only one day to go!' My room is positioned opposite Edinburgh Castle and I open the curtains to the magnificent sight of it in full illumination. I pour myself a juice and sit on my balcony, watching the immense landmark silhouette the night sky. Below me hundreds of voices mark the gathering of youth around the Grass Market nightspots and, after a few reflective moments, I join them.

Anita has flown up this morning and looks tired, the week's events proving a huge emotional strain. She's in good spirits, so we conduct a quick tour of Edinburgh Castle.

We use the rest of the morning to construct the beginning of the show, which Mark has expertly planned as a take-off of the *Trainspotting* opening. Because Edinburgh was used as the same backdrop for the film, we are able to duplicate the scenes at the actual locations. Filming takes longer than usual, and we are wrapped up by 5.00pm. Anita catches her return flight and we spend the night packing before going out for a celebration drink with Johanna at a nearby pub.

I fall asleep with the comforting thought that the first four shows are in the can.

Chapter 11 | MACAU

Day 72, Saturday 20ᵗʰ September

There is an expansive double-glazed window that enables me to see the whole of the Hong Kong harbour from my tiny room at the Kowloon Hotel. Sadly, like most days in this fascinating city, a smoky haze blankets the fine landscape. There is no chance of seeing the next skyscraper let alone catching a glimpse of the horizon.

At 10 o'clock we pass through Gate Number 6 at the Hydrofoil Terminal. Our transport sways slowly in the wake of a passing barge in the form of a Jetfoil, an ugly combination of hovercraft and small vessel, which carries us toward our fifth destination, the Portuguese territory of Macau.

There was some debate, prior to our departure, that the recent spate of Mafia-induced murders may be viewed as an occupational hazard to the filming of the destination, but that concern has long disappeared as I settle back into my Jetfoil First Class seat. I question the need to split the decks into classes as all the seats seem to be designed for small-bottomed Asians, and the only real difference between First and Second classes seems to be a box filled with two 'concrete' biscuits and a bruised orange juice. Still, I'm not paying.

The scenery seems to be non-existent until the shadow of a forbidding skyline lurks on the horizon and, before we know it, we are surrounded by a jungle of skyscrapers that best describes the main features of Macau. For the books, Macau is a small 'big' city made up of three parts – a peninsula and two islands. All three make up 23.5 square kilometres, the city is only an hour away from Hong Kong but predates it by 300 years. It is the first and will be the last European colony in Asia and is the last of Portugal's colonies. With 450,000 people living here, it makes it one of the most densely populated countries in the world.

On our arrival our director, Nigel Carpenter, greets us enthusiastically and introduces Joao and Patrick who will serve as guide and driver for the week. There is no time to spare as we check in to the Grand View Hotel – which certainly lives up to its name. I open to the curtains to a hilly bay background that is South China, and a 45,000 seater soccer stadium and racecourse provide some impressive foreground.

A quick flick through the soft-porn video channel (just to ensure that it's working properly!) and a quick shower before we gather at the Reclamation area – a disused land mass – that is playing host to the 9th World Fireworks Championships. Tonight the Japanese are competing along with the United Kingdom while tomorrow France take on the USA in the ten team competition.

We are warned that the fallout from the exploding sky rockets can harm spectators, but we venture closer to the launch site with our usual reckless abandon. After a short wait of half an hour – in which we entertain ourselves by climbing down unfinished drainage tunnels – the performance begins.

It is supposed to be the biggest and loudest display on earth and it lives up to its fierce billing. Nigel and I get as close as physically possible as the display explodes above us, spraying colour and gunpowder skyward. The noise echoes over the harbour like a tremendous series of thunder strikes and the cheers of delight from spectators are drowned out by the visual and audio symphony. Twenty minutes later we have sore necks and numbed senses, but full marks all round.

It has started to rain lightly which drops the temperature slightly to around 28 degrees, and we travel to Taipa Island to the Karaoke Bar in the New Century Casino to a comfortable air conditioned lounge. If you've seen one karaoke bar, you've seen the lot but the genuine and serious approach to singing in public by the Macaunese is infectious and we are determined to put on a good show.

A few Diet Cokes later, I find myself blasting out the rather cumbersome strains of *American Pie, Love Me Tender* and *Stand By Me,* for the camera of course. I sing the Elvis classic with an older Macaunese woman who is keen to touch my bottom, but I cleverly manoeuvre myself to avoid any more gropes. The crew finishes with a group rendition of *American Pie.*

Macau tends to be busier on Saturday nights than any other time during the week so Nigel has, quite rightly, insisted that we try to capture as much action as possible tonight. Our final stop is the UFO club, one of the top clubs in this part of Asia, and we are entertained by the visiting American DJ. We all start to feel the pinch of a long night and by 3.30am I lay my head to rest.

We have welcomed two new crew members for this segment, Tim Pattinson, our English soundman and Jennifer 'Weather-Centre' Broadbent, the guest presenter. Both celebrate with a buffet breakfast that the hotel is generously offering (no charge!). Joao and Patrick work for the Macau Tourist Board and have quickly accustomed themselves to the Kiwi sense of humour. I feel fresh as a daisy this morning but am largely unprepared for the heat of the morning as the temperature rockets to 31 degrees by 9.00am.

Coloane Island is only 15 minutes away, and is home to the most modern 'ghost town' that any of us have ever seen. Over the hill from the main island motorway junction lies a series of high rise apartment complexes and seaside villas that are empty – void of any tenants. The reason is due to the strength of Chinese culture. They instinctively prefer to live together, in close quarters, on top of each other – a fact that the real estate and property investors obviously didn't consider.

I ask Joao about the price for an apartment.

'$200' he replies.

'A month?' I ask, given that no one lives here.

'A week' he says with much sorrow.

The markets in Macau provide plenty of colour and variation. Joao gives me the opportunity to venture into an incense shop, and have my face shaved by a street-side barber. The latter proves to be an unusual experience as the barber is an eccentric gentleman, whose looks are not far off Mr Myagi from the Karate Kid, who dry shaves your face while an elderly accomplice plays an ancient tune on an equally gnarly violin.

'It sounds like a death march to me..' I stammer with a nervous grin.

My barber smiles back, and then slices off a chunk of my chin. Nigel is in hysterics as I proceed to get carved up unceremoniously, but Steve and Tim capture the moment in their typical vigilant fashion. The scene is surreal. A barber, a musician, and a bunch of crones playing mahjong in the background. Great television.

When we shot the Hong Kong show, Steve had trouble filming in the fish and meat markets due to the refusal of some patrons to allow the

Jennifer "Weather-Centre" Broadbent
and Nick, Macau.

camera near the stalls. Joao assures us that we won't have these problems as he and I venture into the Ya Ting fish markets. The sight of a frog being skinned alive is not a pleasant one, but to these people it is a custom and occupation. It is not an easy thing to stomach. Like most markets, it is where the locals meet to do the grocery shopping (why someone needs a skinned frog is beyond me!) but after the 'defrogging' I decide that fresh food comes a close second to hamburgers.

Gambling is the number one cash cow in this town, with many billions changing hands every year. About 40% of government revenue comes from gambling, and with 8 casinos it is easy to see why Macau is known as the Las Vegas of Asia. Another pulse of income is horse and dog racing, and the latter is our destination tonight. We are doubtful that the camera will be allowed in the casinos so this will be the closest to gambling we get to.

The Macau Canidrome Dog Races is a chance for me to lay a few dollars on the mutts but I have no luck. Brian Murphy, an Irishman who was asked to set up dog racing in the territory, offers me a useful tip.

'Don't gamble!' he chuckles.

He loves Macau – the good food, the relaxed lifestyle and, despite his vested and professional interest in dog racing, he doesn't gamble although he can relate to the obsessive nature of Chinese gambling.

'If we've got a dollar in our pockets and are hungry we'll spend it on food, if a Chinese person has a dollar in his pocket and is hungry, he'll gamble.' Brian offers.

For purpose of filming, I need to be seen around town with a date on my arm so Nigel arranges for a local girl to join us for a few nights filming. Her name is Agnes Lo and she happens to be the current Miss Macau title holder. She is competing in the Miss World Beauty Pageant in London and achieved a degree from the University of Hawaii. She is taking a year off and plans to travel to Australia to complete her Masters. It is enjoyable talking to her, as the boys giggle in the background, as she has led a life similar to mine. It has been a long day and we have our own private rejoice when Nigel mentions those irrepressible words, 'It's a wrap!'

They have taken away the elegant utensils and full buffet-style breakfast from the previous morning and replaced it with orange scrambled eggs and cold coffee. I knew it was too good to be true. Patrick, our driver, greets us with much enthusiasm (but hardly any English) and takes us away to meet Father Texiera, the oldest living Portuguese resident in Macau. He is supposed to be 85 years old, but when I catch a peak at his gnarled and ancient figure I determine an additional 200 years to that total. He certainly acts like a younger man and takes an instant liking to Jennifer, who interviews him outside the steps of St. Paul's Church.

Father Texiera (pronounced Tey-shee-arr, although we have given him the nickname Ted Shearer) trained in the priesthood at the age of 12 and since that time has written 124 books and writes for two daily papers. He stands about 5 foot 3, with a ghostly white beard that trails to his tummy, he wears a silk cloak and balances on a pine walking stick. It is obvious that this man is a wealth of knowledge, and we take extra time to blood plenty of information from his generous memory.

The backdrop is the Facade – the only remains of a Jesuit Cathedral built in 1602 and attached to a Jesuit College, the first built in Asia. In 1835, a fire started in the college and destroyed both it and the body of the church. Nearby lies a Chinese temple, which in its right is symbolic of the comfortable mix of religions in this town. Conflicting religions around the world lead to death and war while the different religious beliefs in Macau co-exist quite happily.

A group of giggling schoolgirls want me to take a photo, and I expertly shuffle them around to get the perfect shot – much to their amusement. All this religion and photography has given me a ferocious hunger, and I don't have to wait too long before the van pulls up outside Number 4, Da Republica Street on Macau Island. A bright sign appears proclaiming 'Henri's Galley. For Macau's Best, African Chicken, Spicy Prawn and Curry Fresh Crab'. Hmm, yummy.

Nigel had told me that Henri was drunk when he visited the

restaurant during the research week, but even this worthy piece of advice didn't prepare me for this charismatic personality. An Asian version of Ronnie Corbett, Henri greeted us with open arms and a hopelessly infectious laugh, before leading me completely astray in the kitchen. Propped against the wall an official letter from Buckingham Palace was laminated in all its brilliance while numerous awards from International Cuisine Authorities lay about the restaurant. Like most cooks, the kitchen is their battlefield, their domain . . . and even though we managed to conduct an interview, I couldn't help feeling a little intrusive.

'So, what do you think?' Henri asked in his broken English, as I tasted the Portuguese soup. It was beautifully prepared and even more delicious in taste.

'Oh, Henri. It's awesome!'

'Awful?' Much laughter all round.

More laughter is generated among the kitchen workers as I attempt to taste the egg fried rice with a pair of chopsticks. My ineptitude is humorous to the locals. The meal is whisked up within a space of 20 minutes and consists of Portuguese beef and leek soup, egg fried rice, spicy chicken and King Prawns, greens and plenty of drinks. The interview and cooking action is priceless and, together with Henri's accommodating attitude, we are tempted to stay for the rest of the day. Nevertheless, we wave goodbye and head to the Guia Lighthouse for a wide shot of the city – and the haze.

We have a little shooting to do tonight but it is over by 9.00pm, and the hands are raised for Pizza Hutt. Before we leave for the hotel Joao takes me aside and asks if I want to see the 'fish tanks'.

I look at him quizzically and wonder if he has morbid fascination with eels and sharks. He explains by taking me to the fourth floor of the casino building we have just been filming and ushers me behind a large screen. The 'fish tank' is a large one-way mirror that enables the punter to view the 'fish' – half naked Asian prostitutes. By the busload. For research purposes, Joao informs me that the price for an hour is around 1000 Hong Kong dollars ($NZ 200) and then shows me the room full of Koreans and Vietnamese. It is eye-bulging stuff and I eagerly tell the lads when I return.

Pizza is magnificent, and the night reaches its finale with Miss Macau driving me home. Joao has been encouraging me to ask Agnes out on a date but I fumble around the question and end up giving in to the sleepiness that forces me into bed.

Aren't I pathetic? Agnes has a boyfriend anyway. He fixes computer consoles. And he's probably really ugly.

Lou Lim Iok Gardens are only 10 minutes away from our hotel on Taipa, and provide a little oasis in the middle of the hussle and bussle of the big city. In the early morning hours, hundreds of locals come to perform tai chi, prayer and meditation to prepare for the day ahead. It is a true Chinese garden modelled on the famous classical Chinese gardens of Soochow together with stone carvings and intricate foliage design. The gardens were built by a wealthy Chinese merchant in the 19th century, but when he ran out of cash the garden fell into ruin. Luckily the government stepped in, restored it and opened it to the public in 1974.

Among the countless locals who are swaying rhythmically to their music, there lies an old bridge that resembles a serpent, with nine separate turns and corners. The reason for this design is that evil spirits travel in straight lines and cannot possibly cross the bridge!

Due to an overdose of late nights and lagers, Joao is ill in bed so we must make do without his generous charm or, more significantly, his ability to communicate with the locals.

One thing that we have noticed since our arrival is the incredible amount of construction work going on within the city limits. There seems to be a new building under construction on every corner, with the typical bamboo scaffolding networking its way around the concrete masses. Tim is convinced that he could make millions from a new bamboo scaffolding business in New Zealand. Hmmm . . . no.

There is a famous footballing chant in Britain that is often sung when the crowd spots an overweight player or spectator. It is sung to the old favourite *Knees Up Mother Brown*:

'Who ate all the pies? Who ate all the pies?

You fat bastard, you bastard, you ate all the pies!'

Well, if this was sung to any crew member on this pleasant sunny afternoon, it would be me. Me, after we visited Lord Stow's Bakery – the creator of the famous Macau Egg Tart – on Coloane Island. The man behind the famous pie is Andrew Stow, an expatriate Englishman who opened his first shop in 1989 and has experienced phenomenal success with his mixture of egg custard and flaky pastry.

He is a real character who nonetheless finds Macau to be a bit of a bore when compared to the bright lights of Hong Kong. He is generous with his praise for the Macaunese whom he finds to be friendly and hard-working. His business has expanded to three outlets, one in Coloane and two in Macau plus a factory that needs to function for 24 hours to enable adequate supply.

I add three kilos to my waistline as I munch on several pies in the bus. The other crew members find them to be too sweet but that doesn't stop Steve from squeezing in two – at once.

'God, these are beautiful aren't they?' I ask.

'I don't know,' says Nigel. 'You've eaten them all.'

The weather has deteriorated, to our benefit, as the temperature drops to a reasonable level: 28 degrees. The sweat on the back of my neck has solidified to a salty smear but nothing will deter me from having a good time at our next stop. The Institutodos Despartos de Macau is a large go-kart track that was built only a couple of years ago to supply the expected tourist surge that never happened. It still is an impressive complex and we are told by Patrick that it hosts the professional go-kart Grand Prix during the summer. The track runs for about a kilometre, and hosts more turns and chicanes than a Formula One circuit – well, nearly. The starting positions are marked out, and spectators are even supplied with flags to start races.

The karts are hired out for 10 minutes and extra time is charged onto the account, which some higher authority is taking care of. I pick the Number 7 'grunter' and squeeze into the fibreglass seat – the effect of the pies prevents a comfortable fit – and make full use of the acceleration and brake pedals as I hoon around for a couple of practice laps. My opponents for the race today are two Aussie chefs, Craig and Greg, who work at the Bella Vista and the Mandarin Hotels respectively. Both establishments are very classy, and they are treated well by the patrons and employers which gives them adequate time and money to spend.

The Trans Tasman rivalry is obvious as we rev the engines and, on the first turn, we all spin out at the corner with Craig flipping in a full 360 degree crash. There is a moment of concern as he untangles himself from the wreckage but he eliminates the possibility of any damage by jumping straight into a reserve car. I take the chance to race ahead. Realistically, they are far better than I am so, in a supreme act of diplomacy, we decide to race it out over 2 laps and it ends up climaxing into a three kart sprint for the finish line. The victory, sadly, goes in favour of the Australians and a champagne shower is all I get in return.

The Chinese mechanic isn't very pleased with the damage we have done to his karts. I have dismembered a brake disc while Greg and Craig have both over-heated the engines. No surprise as Tim later tells me later that we have been racing for well over 2 hours. I am covered in bruises and oil but thrilled at the chance to race for New Zealand, albeit badly.

Boys just want to have fun when it comes to adventure, so on our early morning visit to the Guia Lighthouse we climb down a deserted tunnel shaft with our wits and a bloody good torch the only companions. Nigel spots lizard eggs, while Steve spots a lizard. I hang off Tim's belt in fear there is a monster living at the end of this little trek. Ultimately, the tunnel leads nowhere but the boys get frightened when Steve runs off with the torch, plunging us into darkness. I think I heard Nigel whimper in fear.

The promise of a free swim attracts us immediately to the Western Hotel on Coloane Island, where we do some promotional work for the Tourist Board. The hotel is virtually empty (another sign of Coloane Island's lack of appeal) but is remarkably well kept. The swimming pool is luxurious and the gymnasium equipment looks as if it has been untouched by human hand.

We are scheduled to jet-ski at midday but, due to some adventurous driving on the nearby beach, we manage to get our trusty van stuck fast in the sand. Plenty of scratching of heads before the arrival of a bulldozer to drag our supply vehicle to safety. The owner of the jet-ski hire is rather reluctant to let us in the water (apparently the waves are too high), but we convince him that I am an expert hand at jetskiing – an utter lie.

The sensation of jumping through waves is heightened by a school of fish, who keep me company throughout my numerous circuits of the bay. After an exhausting hour at sea, Nigel wants a final shot of presenter passing company with his machine and I plough head on into a breaking waves and knock myself cold.

I have had a number of concussions during my rugby playing days, but this is only mild in comparison. An immense feeling of disorientation sweeps over me, and Steve is quick to carry my flailing body out of the surf, and into the safety of a shelter. I feel sick and the overwhelming need to throw up overcomes me.

'I don't want to go to hospital. Don't want to go to the hospital' I repeat, subconsciously.

After an hour, I am able to walk back to the van. That night I am shown footage of my ocean adventure and I struggle to remember any of it. A sore head prevents a good night's sleep. At the end of the day, it makes great television and that pleases me no end.

We bumped into a Kiwi lass at the dog racing on Monday who worked as a groom at the Macau Jockey Club and so Jennifer, Tim, Steve and Nigel meet her for a quick chat about life in Macau. Much like Brian Murphy, she enjoys the relaxed lifestyle and the food but is still a New Zealander at heart. Her skills with horses are much appreciated by the Macaunese jockeys.

Due to Nigel's fantastic ability to shoot a show in only a few days, the day is set aside for shopping in Hong Kong and I make the mistake of thinking that my body can handle the heat and hype of the big city after yesterday's shenanigans. As soon as the jetfoil docks into the Ferry Terminal, I feel lightheaded and queasy – not the kind of state you want to be in when entering the claustrophobic atmosphere of downtown Honkers. I do the fastest transport turnaround in history, and catch the next trip home.

The rest of the day is spent watching television, and ignoring the fact that the first blue sky in months can be seen outside of my window. I have eaten all the free fruit that they deposited in my room, and so I settle for an American hotdog from room service.

The shopping expedition returns and everyone is proud of their achievements. The Shanghai Tang proves to be a popular stop for the TV3 crew. Again.

Nigel has purchased some double happy fire crackers for the end set-up for the show, and so the Reclamation Area provides the backdrop for our piece of television. Our filming only requires a fuse, so there are about two whole mats of double happies that need to be used – despite the fact that they are illegal in Macau. We light one mat and observe the explosions with deep guffaws, while the second mat does a good job of unexpectedly jumping into Nigel's face as it explodes. A few anxious moments as Nigel is thrown back by the gunpowder. A few nasty but relatively harmless burns under his chin will make a fine trophy.

Unlike most travel days, we get several hours after breakfast to pack and check out of our hotel. Apart from a quick trip to the Westin Resort to pick up some extra shots, we all get a reasonable sleep-in and I receive ample time to begin the complicated process of packing. Most travellers can relate to the various tricks performed in order to lighten bags and fit ridiculous amounts of luggage into a hand-bag sized satchel. After throwing away unnecessary items such as boarding passes, empty boxes, used batteries, old cotton buds and foreign coins, I have a reasonably balanced travel bag.

When it comes to 'real' packing, I always have sympathy for the crew – especially Steve – who have between 10 – 14 metallic cases full of highly fragile and expensive gear that needs to be packed meticulously to avoid breakage. We all muck in when it comes to carrying it around, but some poor sod has to pack it.

Van leaves the hotel at 2.00pm and, following the usual customs problems, we are away by 3.00pm and at the airport by 5.00pm. Despite the fact that we have travelled through Hong Kong's Kai Tak International airport approximately 24 times in the last 10 months, the airline representatives always appear dumbfounded when we ask to check in baggage that far exceeds their flight limit. Due to these misunderstandings, we are almost always delayed and it annoys Steve immensely.

Singapore is shrouded in darkness when Flight CX715 touches down. Our guide is called Mavis and she greets us with a shy smile, even though we are too knackered to look or sound enthusiastic about being in her country. A stifling wall of heat knocks us to our senses as we step outside into the car park and by the time I arrive at the minibus I am dripping in sweat.

'Is it usually this hot?' I ask our tiny guide.

'The haze has made it like this. It is only 31 degrees outside.'

The haze she refers to is the dreaded Asian concoction of atmospheric mist and pollution that drifts over the likes of Malaysia, Indonesia and Singapore every twenty months. This year's 'fog' has been more concentrated due to bush fires in nearby countries, to point where several deaths have been recorded.

'ONLY 31?' I chuckle.

'Yes, but the humidity level is up to 94%' she states methodically.

That is a frightening statistic. Mavis informs us that all TV channels carry a permanent pollution monitor graphic on the corner of the screen.

This is one of first things I observe when I check into Room 203 at the Regalis Court Motel. The second observation is that the temperature in my room is higher than the thermometer outside so I wallop the air-conditioner into action. It is way past midnight at this point and, as I slide into a light snooze, the phone rings and Rob MacLaughlin (this week's director) is at a local night club. I greet him and then pass on a knowledgeable piece of advice regarding my tired state.

'Rob, it's really great to speak to you but can you piss off. Please?'

CHAPTER 12 | **SINGAPORE**

Day 79, 27th September

Singapore breakfast television is a serious affair, but the wooden performance by their presenters makes it quite comical. The air conditioning unit has turned my room into a refrigerator so I make full use of the fluffy duvet and bury myself until our wake up call.

The Cinnamon Room is where we gather and have breakfast, despite the fact that we share this small 'closet' of a room with every other guest. The simultaneous 'munching' of corn flakes causes me to laugh out loud. Stern looks from everyone.

Mavis turns up in our mini-bus and we scurry from 17 degree rooms to 32 degree courtyard to 17 degree air-con bus. The change of temperature is playing hell with our body's equilibrium, so we ensure we drink plenty of fluid during the day. Before lunch, we stop at Arab Street – an area that boasts the highest concentration of shops in the Arab quarter. The pavements prove to be an obstacle course of carpets, cloth, baskets and bags while the shopkeepers do their best to haggle us into action. No reply from the Westerners.

The Singapore Tourist Board is kindly financing our lunch, so in true diplomatic fashion we end up stuffing our faces full of Chinese cuisine – including a traditional seafood mix, scallops and egg white and prawns and chicken. It also gives us the opportunity to catch up with news from home and welcome Lynette Forday to the 'tour'.

To celebrate our magnificent lunch we take the aerial cable car across the harbour to the paradise island of Sentosa. The view from the 75 metre high cable car is picturesque, and the 10 minute trip gives Steve the chance to shoot Singapore from on high.

Sentosa is an island theme park that accommodates a mono-rail system, various native bush reserves, shops and food courts, mini-golf and fairground rides plus a number of resorts lining the waterfront. On this particular morning it is overrun by tourists who swelter in the high humidity, and we are stuck in the middle of the mad rush. I get to use my camera for the first time on the trip, and the view finder immediately fogs up as I expose it to the outside conditions.

A wander down Sunset Bay and a cool drink on Siloso Beach is the first assignment. The beach is beautifully kept with rows of shrubbery and bush manicured perfectly into the golden sand. Beach volleyball is more popular than swimming here, and it's not hard to see why. Twenty metres off shore lie a series of shark and pollution nets, and the forbidding 'Swim at your own risk' signs that litter the beach give you a feeling of insecurity. A Diet Coke only temporarily puts dehydration at bay before I continue to sweat buckets.

The night falls on Sentosa but the darkness is only temporary as the light display from the Musical Fountain brightens up the night sky. The resplendent Merlion – an 18-metre high statue of a Lion – provides the backdrop for the half hour light and water display at the fountain. I start to doze, not through boredom, but by the soothing jets of water that zig zag through the dancing beams of red and orange light. The display tells the story of the rise of Singapore as a nation, and the thundering sound-track adds power to this free-to-public display.

Two of the most popular nightclubs in Singapore, Zouk and Phuture, are situated in the same building which gives us the best of both worlds. The latter has hosted a whole array of famous mixers including Boy George, Danny Rampling and Massive Attack, and tonight we get the chance to boogie into the early hours. The security patrol is almost too polite, as we are greeted and farewelled with massive grins and waves. Sure beats punches and headbutts.

We got in this morning at 2.00am, so an early call by Rob is about as welcome as a fart in a spacesuit. The Singapore Good Morning television show has me in stitches after the host forgot to turn his microphone on, and with that I giggle myself out of bed.

Lynette has the morning off, while Chinatown beckons me into its seedy midst. While not an obvious tourist haunt, it really is the true blue market place. Pots of live turtles and fish litter the floor while elderly men toil away behind their respective shop fronts.

A group of female fishmongers give me the chance to scale a fish (or should it be de-scale?) and they laugh at my efforts. Another gentleman insists that I carve a papaya, which I do while listening to his rantings in pidgin English.

'You Kiwi's are yummy' he laughs.

'Always soft this time of year!'

I'm not sure how this comment should be taken, as we make attempts to look tough by puffing out our chests and remind him that New Zealanders are a hardy species. Or perhaps he meant our native bird.

'Not you Kiwis. These Kiwis!' he exclaims, holding up a familiar furry fruit.

There is no need to stop for breakfast as the generous locals insist on offering samples of their produce. My carry bag strains under the weight of papayas, Braeburn apples, marinated beef, spicy chicken, watermelon and mineral water. Not surprisingly, we fill up quickly.

While the local Chinese in this area are surrounded by produce markets, they tend to gather at hawker centres when it comes to eating. One such centre is Maxwell Market, a sprinkling of local eateries serving all manner of Asian takeaways including a very special local serving called the dough stick – a pastry stick cooked in oil and served with instant coffee.

Keeping with the international setting of Chinatown, we take the main road east to Little India and film outside Sri Veeramakaliamman Temple and it certainly proves to be a little piece of India right in the heart of Singapore – it mounts a full-on assault on the senses. All sights, sounds and smells. Steve and I compare it to the heaving mess of New Dehli in the real India, not a thrilling experience.

Most large cities tend to incorporate an underground transport system of some kind and Singapore is no exception. The MRT (Mass Rapid Transit) is probably the easiest (and coolest) way of getting around the city and for a system that is constantly active, it seems to be remarkably clean. The reason for this becomes obvious as we enter the Brabbell station doors – large plastic signs indicating no smoking, no eating, no drinking and, strangely enough, no durians (a native fruit that stinks to high heaven) – are everywhere. Once we commute to Somerset, a few stops down the track, a stuffy railway official stops us and proceeds to gabble to Mavis in high pitch Chinese.

Apparently Lynette was spotted drinking the last drops of her coffee as she was walking into the underground, and has been reported to the station officials. Mavis immediately removes her diplomacy mask and takes on the role of Hulk Hogan, as she gets increasingly irritated by this 'trivial incident'. Rob is swinging punches also.

'Do you realise what we're doing here?' he shouts, as the official gets a free blow dry courtesy of Angry Director. 'We are encouraging people to come here and use your underground. What kind of treatment is this?'

The rest of the crew huddle in the background.

'You'll be okay,' I comfort Lynette. 'You'll get out in 6 years.'

The evening darkness soaks up the remaining light and we wander down Orchard Road, the main street that hosts most of the city's nightclubs and top class department stores. We are momentarily diverted into Planet Hollywood, the movie theme restaurant, and are treated to a free feed. Sadly, an hour earlier, I had opted for a meal at the hotel and missed out on hamburgers, fries and whopping great milkshakes.

I wake from a deep sleep. I had dreamed of playing tennis with Russian sensation Anna Kournikova. It was a great dream. I tell the crew, but they are all suffering after a night of free beer and burgers.

In the middle of this urban jungle there is a real jungle – the Singaporean Zoological Gardens is an open zoo that lies only 40 minutes out of the centre of town. It is an open zoo, which allows the smaller animals to roam free while the larger, more dangerous creatures live behind moats and rivers. The open atmosphere allows visitors to take close photographs with the orang-utan and snakes, while the seals and polar bears can be fed by hand.

Please don't feed the animals.
Singapore Zoo.

The scene reminds me of Jurassic Park, and we are all enthralled at the close vicinity that we achieve with the camera. Steve is delighted with his images: rhinos fighting, lions roaring, tigers sleeping, and two hippos engaging in sexual intercourse (probably won't make the final cut!)

Gene Yam guides us around the park on a small golf cart, and we take time to sample the Cool Rest air-conditioning shelters that are spread over the route. It

One is a wild, savage beast with a silky smooth approach. The other is a python.

gives you some indication as to the high humidity levels in this country (today it has crept up to 94%) that shelters are set up to cater for the lesser tourists. Rob has to coax us out of the comfort with the promise of a 'jungle burger' at the zoo restaurant.

I relish the thought of processing my photographs. Me with a python and a family of orangutans, great for the mantelpiece.

Because Singapore is spread over such a small area, it is often difficult to venture out of the city without falling into the ocean. But today our director has decided to take us on an outing – we must have been behaving ourselves. We gather at Changi Village and catch a bumboat out to the nearby island of Pulau Ubin.

The three wise monkeys.

The trip only takes 15 minutes, and costs a mere $1.50 each way, and even though we travel a small way, it's nice to be out of the city. The boat's captain lets me drive the vessel for a few minutes. It took a while for him to trust me, but he takes one look at the camera before exclaiming:

'I'm gonna be a movie star!'

'Shut up and give me instructions,' I scream as another bumboat brushes our side.

Pulling ashore in Palau Ubin is like stepping back in time to how Singapore looked only 20 years ago. There are wooden shacks sprinkled over this island, housing some of its 600 inhabitants, and I cannot see a single shopping mall in site. An old man grins from his bicycle hire shop, while two playful puppies jog up and down the road.

Apparently the best way of getting around is on the a mountain bike ($6 hire) or in a cheap rusty cab. With camera gear and sound equipment to transport, we opt for the second alternative and, following a bumpy ride around the coast, we are collected by a small jet boat that shunts us onto a floating fishing colony or 'keelong'.

The wind is warm and refreshing and it has dispersed the haze downstream, revealing a hilly expanse on the opposite side of this inlet. Mavis points out that this is better known as Malaysia.

It looks like a scene from *Apocalypse Now*, and I am almost expecting to hear the dull thud of combat helicopters approaching over the horizon. The 'keelong' acts as a floating home to 5 fishermen, who catch and farm large schools of fresh fish to be sold on the mainland. It is obvious that they are not used to visitors – in particular Kiwi film crews – and they immediately retire to their quarters. There are three dogs keeping watch, and their constant barking also proves they are not accustomed to strange faces or smells.

Rob's plans have been mixed up in translation, and the original idea of Lynette and I participating in the process of executing a catch is lost when it's revealed that the net is operated mechanically. Lights are switched on under the water, which attracts the fish, and the net is hauled up by a generator. The catch is significant but most of the fish will be farmed in the underlying pools until they grow large enough to be exported.

Lynette Forday on the wharf.

The fishermen are not fluent in any language it seems and Lynette tries valiantly to strike up a conversation with the head honcho while cooking up some of the catch.

'So do you know how to cook fish many different ways?

'Huh?'

'Do you have any seasoning for this?'

'Huh?'

'Or herbs to bring out the taste?'

'Huh?'

'You must get lonely out here?'

'Huh?'

'Oh God, don't bother.'

It is pitch black now and we can't wait to get off the keelong and back onto the mainland. It was worth the trip and we have managed to capture some great television. The idea of being alone on that island is somewhat disturbing and we dreaded being their next victims. We have a late meal and a drink before retiring. Smelling of fish.

We need to film inside one of the hotel rooms for an item on accommodation but, like most things in this country, you need permission from hundreds of officials so it takes some time before we get a positive answer.

It is National Children's Day in Singapore which means our visit to the Jurong Bird Park is accompanied by thousands of primary school children in little pink raincoats. They all wait patiently in the main amphitheatre at the JBP Bird Park for the show to begin. Sadly, due to a torrential downfall, it is delayed for several hours so the only consolation is a muffled melody over the intercom. In the light of such events, we always have a back-up plan . . . go shopping.

Raffles City Shopping complex houses plenty of fixed price items which limits any haggling potential, but prices are still staggeringly low. New video cameras at $400, minidisc walkman at $350, CDs for as low as $4 etc. No-one in the crew is keen enough to separate with any sizeable amount of dosh but browsing can be good for the soul, and we walk with extra spring as we leave.

Surprisingly, the rain has caused the haze to lift, and suddenly there are more buildings than before. With tummies rumbling we search out a worthy eatery. Having been in Asia for over 12 days we yearn for some

Western sustenance and find solace in 'The Sandwich Bar'. Which had a bar. And sold sandwiches.

Back to Jurong for a second take at the Bird Show. Hooray, success! No clouds, just sun as the flamingos, cranes and parrots perform various acts to the delight of the enthusiastic crowd. Several cockatoos ride bicycles and one clever bird sings 'Happy Birthday' into the microphone. I sit back and take photos with the big publicity camera, while Lynette nurses a sparrow on her shoulder.

The Bird Show encourages audience participation, which gives license to a collection of high pitched squeals from excited children, and Rob. The afternoon is concluded with a trip on the monorail system that circumnavigates the park, providing a view that captures the real size of a nature reserve of this magnitude. It is surprising to read a large sign at the entrance:

'This is an open air park. With the exception of a number of endangered species, most of the wildlife within the confines of this reserve is free roaming. Birds may enter and leave without restraint.'

A satay chicken feast is washed down with a cold mineral water, and then I return to the hotel. The sensation of slipping out of sticky clothes and into a refreshing shower is priceless. Seeing the grime and sweat wash down the plug hole gives you an idea of how much pollution we are swimming in every time we step outside the door.

I am standing on the front steps of one of the most expensive hotels in the world. Raffles Hotel was never on the list of accommodation options for this crew but it is worth the visit. A marketing representative shows us the various suites, and I have the dubious honour of traipsing through the Raffle Suite – temporary quarters of Elizabeth Taylor, Michael Jackson and Madonna. Asking price for one night? $6,000 plus extras.

Raffles houses up to 300 different rooms – all varying sizes and prices – together with several restaurants and conference areas, and the tourist-friendly haunt of the 'Long Bar'. I jump across into the bar area and make a 'Singapore Sling' with a friendly waiter, and serve it to my long suffering crew. The 'Sling' is made up of a concoction of spirits, crushed ice, strawberry juice and fruit and, although highly alcoholic, it has a pleasant taste and several are demolished.

The only item left unticked on my programme rundown is the

outdoor Chinese Opera which is held at Clarke Quay in the centre of the city. Sufficiently full of cafes and restaurants, the quay is beginning to swarm with party goers and young couples, preparing for a night on the town. The Chinese Opera is performed on a makeshift platform and attracts a reasonable crowd, who clap appreciatively at every movement. The camera rolls for a few minutes, and then Rob decides to call it quits.

We finish the night with a fine Italian meal courtesy of Mavis and the Singapore Tourist Association at the 'Al Dente Trattoria'. Pizza, pasta and tiramisu are ordered and devoured, and we toast the fine work of Steve Orsbourn who has completed his 16th and final show. Plenty of laughing and merriment, although Lynette's black coffee took nearly 20 minutes to make.

There is considerable doubt this morning that we are booked onto the correct flight and the confusion is complimented by the Hotel fire alarm roaring into action at 4.00am. Sadly, this leads to a fault with the elevator and all 18 cases have to be dragged down three flights of stairs – mostly by Steve. The utterly banal process of checking in luggage and sorting out transfers is lessened by the sight of home on the horizon. Rob is missing his wife desperately, as is Steve with his partner, and I just want to have a hot bath when I get back.

Flight CX714 leaves Singapore, and I'm sure I can see Mavis waving from my Business Class seat. She really was a sweetie, and I'm sure she'll never come across a bunch of idiots like us again. Until next series perhaps.

CHAPTER 13 | SWITZERLAND

Day 85, Thursday 23rd October

My Business Class tickets sit safely in my trouser pocket as the Cathay Pacific stewardess serves me the biggest bowl of pistachio nuts I have ever seen. Not wanting to offend her gracious service I promptly demolish the entire serving before realising that half of them were yet to be 'unshelled'.

Twenty-six hours later, my weary eyes adjust their gaze from the personal television set to the majestic sight of the Swiss Alps peaking a number of cheeky summits through the low flying cloud. Beneath us lies the city of Zurich, population 356,000 that swells by several thousand during the ski season.

In usual fashion, the hotel rooms aren't ready until midday so we acquaint ourselves with the city streets. Eventually we gather with Rob McLaughlin, our director, to discuss the shoot. Much to our disdain, he has organised an official meal with Tourist Board representatives tonight. Although promised to end at 10.00pm, it drags long into the night.

We get our early call from Rob at 4.00am after only two torrid hours of sleep. Beyond the safe confines of my double glazed window on the hotel 3rd floor, the city awakens slowly. The Liebenstrasse (main street) slowly transforms itself into a hive of activity as the bright sunshine melts away the morning mist and adds colour to the concrete and cobblestoned streets of Zurich.

Several days previous, Rob McLaughlin and I had strolled along Orchard Road in downtown Singapore – exhausted and drained from the crippling humidity. Yet now, in the middle of neutral Europe, the fresh, cool breeze of a northern hemisphere autumn is more therapeutic than uncomfortable and serves as a more efficient wake-up burst than any alarm clock.

It becomes immediately obvious from the cleanliness, upmarket shopping facilities and classy dress sense and aloof demeanor of the locals that Zurich is an affluent city. One of the hotel concierges informed me that the average wage in the city is equivalent to NZ$36,000. A higher standard of living, mixed with the Swiss' urgent and efficient approach to tourism and self promotion, means there is an obvious absence of buskers, beggars or homeless – together with no visual evidence of graffiti or litter. Lower socio-economic groups would find it difficult to survive, let alone afford, to stay within the city walls.

I have a huge blister on the heel of my left foot which is somewhat bewildering, considering I have not participated in any running or exercise that usually encourages this. I hobble with the rest of the crew down the main street.

The Swatch and Swiss Army knife shops prove to be popular haunts for the tourist population and the DPE crew is no different. Tony comes across a Swiss Army knife with more than 200 attachments but nearly swallows his tongue when he discovers its NZ$1,000 price tag. Belinda Todd expresses interest in the Swatch collection while Rob and I eye up a new pair of Oakley sunglasses called 'Romeo'.

These outlets provide an opportunity to view for personal and professional interests, together with a quick walk down the street talking to some of the local characters. We come across two co-operative policemen who agree to talk to the camera. Both individuals are proud to be involved in the process of upholding a reputation of a virtually crime-free city. As usual I quiz them relentlessly about their jobs and watch as they freely demonstrate the use of their guns and truncheons. In the country that proudly boasts an abundance of international bank accounts and more reserves of monetary power than any other, there is one real question to ask:

'So guys, with so many banks in close proximity, isn't there any concern over crime?'

'No,' one of them replies. 'Only burglary.'

The bewildering difference in nationalities and language in Switzerland stems from the multi-national proverb that 'there is no such thing as a true Swiss'. This is evident when it comes to the dark beauty and fiery temperament of the Swiss-Italian, the blond Arian colour and efficiency of the Swiss-German, together with the passion and dark features of the Swiss-French provides a real cosmopolitan mix of looks, behaviour and attitudes.

During the research week for this destination, Rob and Coral Barrett (researcher) had encountered a number of difficulties in organisation due to the lethargic response of the local authorities. This wasn't due to a lack of enthusiasm or persuasiveness on the part of the Tourist Commission but a necessary adherence to efficiency and executing actions 'by the book'.

Belinda and I take a short stroll up the Lindinhoff Gardens for the best view of the Old Town buildings, and to participate in an impromptu game of chess with some local gentlemen. The Lindinhoff Gardens also provide a wide, expansive garden area in which to sit and soak up the ambience of a panoramic view of the city university and fast-flowing river.

Our two new crew members, Tony Wilson and Matt Heine seem to be enjoying themselves as the day begins to bear fruit in terms of captured footage. There's nothing more satisfying for the man holding the camera than shooting quality footage. The cohesion of a TV crew is imperative to the success of a programme and 'Destination Planet Earth' has been extremely lucky to have had some superb technicians working on this show. Steve Orsbourn, who shot the first 16 shows, has now gone to Australia for the cricket telecast but Tony has quickly slipped into the role without any problem.

At 6.00pm we wearily wander back to the hotel to freshen up before Nicola (our driver) collects us at 8.00pm to start our nightclub excursion. The two nightclubs that Rob has chosen are Adagio and Mascot – the first of which turns out to be a carefully re-constructed ancient medieval chapel with plenty of low light and detailed interior décor ranging from 16th century armour and weaponry to worn wooden pulpits and embroidered curtain decorations.

The music is slow and laboured so when I approach the DJ, he invites me into the music booth to talk. He explains how the music programme starts with a romantic theme and eventually winds up into a disco theme. He plays in clubs for 6 nights a week but claims that it doesn't reward him financially:

'I don't get much. But it's fun. You know, Zurich is a conservative city during the day but it does become more animated at night. Although it does struggle to compete as a bastion of serious dance culture.'

From the DJ booth I notice that the punter's age range varies greatly from the young couples to older professional people – who don't seem too concerned over the youthful vibes of the club – and its refreshing to see everybody enjoying themselves in a non-confrontational atmosphere. There is a touch of irony when Rob announces he is celebrating his wedding anniversary tonight. Alone. On the other side of the world.

The final stop of the day (or early morning!) is the recently opened Mascot nightclub. Modern and clean in appearance, it lacks the ambience of the earlier hot spot. Nevertheless, the 'Flintstones' architecture and 'acid house' music mix livens up the half-empty dance floor and we all complete a hectic day with a leisurely boogie. At 3.00am, Tony and I snail our way through the dingy streets.

I wake from a deep sleep. I had dreamed of playing tennis with Russian sensation Anna. In the nude. Despite falling asleep at nearly 4.00am, I wake wide-eyed and raring to go. The hotel staff greet me with smiles – including the manager who we discover is also an actor (he popped up on CNN last night!) The Central Hotel – as its name suggests – is located right at the heart of the city, in close proximity to the tram station and directly opposite to the main underground shopping complex. Although this is my 16th destination in the last year, I have discovered through experience that it takes a good 48 hours to recover from the exhausting combination of jetlag and peculiar working hours.

The face of a jaded traveller, Zurich.

The change in timezones can drastically alter your sleeping patterns, which promotes a sense of disorientation and discomfort. There are various theories as to how an individual can combat the effects of long-haul travel but everyone swears by different methods. I sleep whenever I feel tired – even if it's in the middle of the day.

The Widder Hotel is famous for its classical architecture and fabulous interior designs. Belinda mixes drinks in the kitchen while I play with the electric windows in a high priced room on offer. While the manager explains the various commercial aspects of the hotel (yawn!) I wander down to the kitchen and bump into the assistant chef Martin Ingold. Although he lacks a fluent knowledge of English, the international cooking language speaks volumes to my hardened kitchen hands.

Roschti, a traditional Swiss snack, is quite simply a large hash brown that is prepared through slicing several potatoes into thin stringy portions. Once formed into a small portion through the aid of eggs and oil, the roschti is fried for about 12 minutes before being served with tomato and spicy seasoning. The nature of this local dish proves to be extremely popular with both Tony and Matt, who dispense with the formality of using a fork and knife and willing shovel my feeble effort into their hungry stomachs.

The shoot schedule has been cast into some disarray when we realise that the hotel visit (only planned for an hour) has lasted almost three. Tempers fray as the pressure of lost time begins to tell on the faces of the director and crew. Filming is temporarily halted while we collect our thoughts over a pepperoni pizza at Sam's Kitchen in the Barnhoff Strausse. Due to the European autumn sun setting earlier than we are used to in the southern hemisphere, Tony estimates that we lose shooting light by approximately 4.15pm and will need to economise our time more efficiently. There was an abundance of time wasting this morning that has, unnecessarily, lengthened our day.

Only a few hours ago we were eating roschti, minutes ago pizza and now the boys board the Hochechaiser – the city's only tram restaurant. The Eat and Ride theme seems to be quite popular in Zurich and it gives us a chance to enjoy the view as it slowly worms its way through the city. It is a genuine, though hardly unique concept, which seems to entertain more locals than tourists. A meal of venison and milk bread is served with a fruit basket and copious amounts of alcohol. Sure enough, the existing conservative atmosphere develops into a full-blown carnival party. I take the chance to grab the tram microphone and encourage a few verses of the national anthem.

We roll into the Central Hotel at 7.00pm and collect a message that has been left at the desk for me. It reads:

'To the New Zealand film crew, we have a Kiwi chef working downstairs in our restaurant. His name is Chris Lowe and he wants to meet you. Signed the Manager.'

It doesn't take Chris too long to find us. He has been working here for almost two years and dearly misses home. Because I have been in a similar situation, I can sympathise with his longing desire to speak to some fellow countrymen. His endless questioning is quite humorous:

'How did the All Blacks play last week?'

'Who won the National Provincial Championship?'

'Do you guys know if they've built that shopping mall down in Masterton?'

Chris accompanies us to one of the city's trendiest bars, the curiously named Deep Shit. Sadly Deep Shit hasn't got a late license and we're turfed out by midnight.

During the night I have slept on my side, cutting off all the circulation on the left side of my face and left arm. I wake up thinking that I've suffered a mild stroke. I tell the crew of my dilemma, which is greeted by raucous laughter. Thanks guys.

After only two days, we are packing our bags already for a short trip to Lucerne leaving Emile and the friendly Central Hotel staff behind. Although our destination is only 60 minutes away (as the crow flies) Rob has decided to take the scenic route giving Tony the chance to shoot the Swiss villages and rolling landscape. The Tourist Commission treated us to a free English breakfast this morning, but the nasty combination of greasy bacon and eggs together with slow, winding roads encourages my stomach to do somersaults.

The drive proves to be pleasant and we're all staggered with the remarkable resemblance that the Swiss countryside has to New Zealand. The colours are bright, the air crisp and pastureland lush. Approximately 30 km down the road Emile swaps driving duties with a large, bald behemoth of a man called Claude who has in his possession a pair of the largest hands I have ever seen. When shaking his hand, it literally engulfs me. He delivers us to Hotel Des Balance in the heart of the Weinmarket in Lucerne.

After quickly unpacking, we head for Lake Lucerne, and pay 10 Francs for a ride aboard an old paddle steamer. The trip takes an hour and provides an alternative way of absorbing some stunning mountain scenery. Chuckles all round when we are told by the ship's captain Peter Sigrist that the vessel is called 'Sheila' although I am saved ultimate embarrassment when I notice the peeling 'certificate of transit' issued to the 'Maritime Boat: Schiller'. Named after a famous Swiss poet. Apparently.

Peter and his second mate Claus talk willingly to the camera, but I struggle to prompt any outstanding grabs or quotes as they both lack a sense of humour – or is it because I have no sense of worthy interview technique? Gradually they warm to my seamanship and let me steer the boat. I also get the chance to let off steam . . . er, by blowing the horn which gives most passengers a bit of a shock.

The second level of the Schiller boasts a smiling accordion player by the name of Colomba Cannino who is happy to provide backing vocals and musical accompaniment to a rather impromptu version of 'Pokarekareana'.

Sundays in Switzerland, like most places around the world, are quiet and relaxed which does provide certain limitations on what events are operating, what shops are functioning and what tourist attractions are open. Rob decides that we may be in need of an early finish. As we talk, the surrounding majestic mountain range is revealed through a hazy mist and the click of Polaroid cameras is the only sound you hear from the boat's viewing quarters. It is a breathtaking sight.

Claude meets us at Hernserten with the van and we stop at Café Ricci on our return for a quick coffee and an opportunity to watch Mikka Hakkinen win the Spanish Grand Prix.

Before daylight disappears completely, we visit the Lion Monument – an enormous statue carved out of a rock face. Despite my considerable hunger I decide not to go out for dinner with the crew and instead catch up on slumber.

Sleepy and lethargic but keen to get into some work this morning. There is a fantastically funny cartoon series on one of the German satellite channels this morning – Des Simpsons. A German 'Homer' has absolutely no appeal to me. The beautiful girl at reception isn't smiling anymore – in fact she looks as grumpy as sin. In-between croissants I steal gazes out of the dining room window. The misty cloud shrouds the city skyline leaving Rob hesitant about even attempting any wide scenic shots so that option is abandoned.

For some reason, our driver Claude gets more sinister everyday. Belinda has managed to juice some personal information out of our guide – and has deduced that he was once a soldier and mercenary. No doubt more gory details will surface in the next week.

The DPE machine rolls into action at about 9.00am, and Tony has packed all the necessary equipment into the back of the van. Being a cameraman is a thankless job; he clearly carries the most responsibility of the crew and his day never really finishes.

The rest of us pampered souls clamber aboard – an eye warily on Claude (after Belinda's tales) and we head for the Lowenstrausse. Our destination is the Lockheart Swiss Army Knife Shop – owned by a young Swiss Italian woman by the name of Claudia Fresco. It becomes obvious that she is a thorough businesswoman, but also generous enough to explain the variations in knives. Her collection is impressive – ranging from the simplest single bladed 'Tiger' to the monstrous 32-attachment 'Champ' model. The prices are reasonable for such a staggering range. The knives are readily available for sale overseas but not in the white or black colour.

Claudia's charm and deep brown eyes have won over the crew and that seems to be reflected in the number of purchases made. I restrict myself to a Swiss Champ but Tony and Matt have lost count of their buys.

Two hours later, we emerge. I pass the 'presenter baton' to Belinda, who investigates the Picasso Museum – a unique collection of his early works together with a priceless set of real life photographs of the artist. Some of the black and white stills reveal the face of a tortured genius, contorted by the strain of his own expectation. Others show Picasso playfully interacting with his wife and children – the archetypical family portrait. Despite his impending death, he was a remarkably handsome man – grey flecks of hair contrasting against his thick, leathery face. The crew is warned that the walls and paintings are all pressure alarmed with a circuit security system, so our entire tour is spent watching each other desperately trying to avoid leaning on anything. The overload of art and shopping has weighed heavily on the spirit of the boys and we welcome the evening entertainment.

Rob has booked us into the National Transport Museum's IMEX theatre – a huge 70mm cinema complex that houses a massive 50-ft screen. The film is called *Images of the Serengeti* – a mind-blowing documentary which boasts some staggering camera shots.

The performances vary from *Blue Planet* (NASA's shots of Earth), to *Whales* (Maritime Movie). The English narration is provided by James Earl Jones.

There had been plans organised for a visit to a local casino and a cabaret performance but, to our relief, we have been spared the tortuous ordeal – at least until tomorrow. We descend on the Hotel Des Balances hotel bar where a few drinks are consumed. At about midnight the bar shuts and I end up rambling on to the waitress.

Adventure Day is upon us. The schedule says, in bold capitals:

BUNGY, MOUNTAIN CLIMBING,
ABSEILING, GONDOLA RIDING!

Our journey is to the top of Mount Titlis (a name that prompts large quantities of guffawing among the crew) which stands a majestic 3,030 feet. Belinda has been quietly confident all week that she will get the opportunity to ski but Claude is adamant there will be NO snow at a low level on the mountains. Everyone looks several kilograms fatter today due to the heavy clothing we are protecting ourselves with. The chilly Swiss Alp temperature commands plenty of respect.

I am well prepared but have forgotten my gloves and need to borrow Belinda's fluorescent pink numbers. Rob sits cozily between several layers of Gore-Tex/wool/nylon.

The cloud cover is low when we arrive but are promised blue sky at the summit. There are 4 separate gondola trips before we reach the peak but our trip takes a quick detour at the first station. The Gondola Bungy team of Remo, Markus and Antoine greet us with engaging smiles. The concept of this jump is rather bizarre but equally fascinating. Today, we will jump from the 70m section as the low cloud prevents us from going any further.

Claude and Belinda huddle around a coffee machine while the Gondola snails its way through the thick mist as Markus and Antoine harness me onto the bungy cord. About 5 minutes later, there is a loud clunk as the Gondola comes to a grinding halt. I throw a worried stare the way of the DVC camera:

'I can't see the bloody bottom!' I shout.

Rob peers over the edge of the open door and laughs nervously.

'You'd never get me doing that,' he replies.

I have jumped on several occasions but have never felt so unsure about this particular set-up. The low cloud has not dissipated, in fact it's getting lower. The visibility from the top of the bungy cord would be no more than 3 metres. Markus doesn't make things any easier.

They're not paying me enough to leap
out of an aerial gondola and bungy
through a cloud!

'Can you hear that low humming from down below?'

'Yeah?' I answer, quizzically. A large lump appears in my chest.

'Well, you are jumping over another gondola line,' he smiles.

I strain my eyes in the vain hope of catching a glimpse of the Gondola cables but to no avail. I hear it, but I just don't see it. It is the most unnerving of adrenalin sports but is heightened somewhat by the bizarre circumstances.

'5-4-3-2-1 . . . BUNGY!!!!'

No time for second thoughts as I plummet towards *terra firma*. The jump is short and sweet. The thrill of the launch equalled only by the sudden appearance of pine trees to my left and a ski-lift cable to my right. I have a chance to relive the experience twice as we strap the DVC to various parts of my anatomy.

A few hours later – feeling numb around the fingers and toes – we board the remaining gondolas for the steady climb to the summit. The final leg is taken in the ROTAIR – rotating gondola – giving Tony a chance to film the scenery from several interesting angles. With about five minutes to go on our final journey upward, Remo taps me on the shoulder and announces that it will only take 10 more seconds before we rise above the cloud line and see the mountain ranges.

Sure enough, the ROTAIR creeps through the last of the low cloud to reveal several snow-covered peaks and the huge blue expanse of a cloudless sky. Sunglasses are suddenly put to use as the glare increases. The first step out of the Gondola is onto fresh snow – something I haven't experienced for at least seven years. Belinda appreciates the view while Remo and I drive a few golf balls off the summit of Mount Titlis. He assures me that we are teeing off into Italy.

The next hour is spent feasting on pizza and riding plastic sleds down

156

the mountain. The air is thin and we poke fun at Rob when he suddenly feels light-headed: lack of fitness, perhaps? He gets a phone call from his wife on his mobile. From Auckland to the Swiss Alps. Amazing.

The trip down is not as spectacular. We are knackered from the day's adventures but still have to endure a Swiss Folklore Show that is, quite frankly, appalling. A collection of old crusties trying to make music with brooms, horns and bells. Belinda and I try to convince Rob to pack up and go home. So appalling is the performance, that I decide to take up smoking. Claude is amused.

'You've never smoked before? No?'

'Never mate.'

'Well don't start asking for my bloody fags!'

Returned to Zurich this morning. Had a ride on a cheese bike – cost about NZ$17.00 for a half day. Plenty of people wanting to hire bikes at the station which gives some sort of indication as to the popularity of cheese bikes. During filming I nearly hit a poor pedestrian who shouted abuse in German.

The rest of the afternoon is spent looking in shop windows. I think the prices are quite expensive and only resort to buying a handful of presents for the family.

'Hey, Eynon! Are you up yet? We're waiting for ya!'

Rob's voice seems a million miles away. It sounds like he's calling my name from the bottom of my toilet. Much confusion until I realize the hotel phone has fallen onto the ground and, next thing I know I'm desperately trying to procure the hand piece. My vision is blurred and my head is thumping. My recollections of the previous night's activities are vague, and it suddenly dawns on me that I must be suffering the effects of a hangover.

Disgust is replaced by guilt as I come to terms with my first alcoholic binge. I have never consumed more than a sip of beer (when I was a 10-year-old) and have been proudly maintaining my abstinence for the last 14 years. As I cast an exhausted eye over the empty contents of the minibar, I grasp the pathetic nature of my actions. I have managed to drink seven bottles of Kronenburg and several spirits, and have left my hotel bedroom in a real state of disarray.

After years of trying to relate to my friends' alcohol-induced moods, I can now understand what is meant by 'beer-breath', 'hangover' and feeling 'dog-rough', after this rather first hand experience. It will be the first and last time I bother with the contents of my hotel refrigerator.

'Are you okay?' asks Rob, as I open my door to the disaster within.

'Um, no. I think I got pissed last night.'

'Oh, well. There's always a first time.'

Rob is good enough to help out with the cleaning effort, and I retire beneath the covers for a healthy dose of sleep. The crew have the chance to view a local chocolate factory while I recover from my evening's indulgence. The day provides sporadic slumber plus a few appalling German movies, and then room service to cap off one of the worst days of my young life.

Typically, the day blossoms early sunlight and the mist lifts to reveal the kind of scenery so often associated with Swiss postcards and tourists pamphlets. Sadly, the camera has been packed away and these fabulous scenes are wasted on memories, not celluloid.

Departure from the hotel is effortless, although my hotel bill is considerably larger than usual. We leave at 10.00am and then fly out of Europe at 1.30pm.

CHAPTER 14 | CHIANG MAI, THAILAND

Day 94, Saturday 1ˢᵗ November

I often talk about the effects of long haul travel – you're probably sick to death of me going on about it! I have made a mental note of the success ratio that we have for travelling in Business Class and discover that 95% of our journeys are made at the upper end of the plane.

To most punters it may seem that business class offers extraordinary luxury – believe me, after travelling economy for so many long haul flights I think we are very lucky – but, more importantly, it offers a travelling film crew the only opportunity to rest and recuperate before the next shoot. It is often noted in our shoot schedule that 'travelling day is rest day'.

So what does business class offer that economy doesn't?

Extra leg space, reclining seat, choice of four main meals and quality service can often prove to be the difference between a relaxing slumber and battery recharge or an uncomfortable cramped trip down in economy. However, no matter whether you're seated in the toilet or the cockpit, you still can't escape the fact that we all travel in the same can of sardines for over 12 hours.

People deal with the trips differently. Rob struggles to sleep while I find it easy to doze in any position – a bag full of sleeping pills can often help the situation.

We arrive at Bangkok International Airport at exactly 12.15pm. The Airport Authorities entertain us with a thorough refusal to accept our 18 pieces of gear for the internal flight to Chiang Mai. Tony experiences some communication problems with the customs officers who fail to co-operate to our meagre demands – another situation that may well have been avoided if the proper organisational ground work had been employed before we left New Zealand. They feel it necessary to charge up to 100 baht (NZ$4) per extra kilogram of luggage exceeding their domestic limit. Considering we carry over 400kgs, Tony would have to dig deep.

Eventually common sense prevails on part of the Thai officials and we board Thai Airways Flight Number 21 for an hour journey north to our ultimate destination. We all sleep comfortably in the cramped economy section and feel considerably relieved when the wheels hit the runway. Mark Everton greets us enthusiastically and I offer my hand in my marriage when he tells us that the next 2 days are free of any filming.

The accommodation is superbly provided by the Chiang Mai Plaza Hotel, hosting a gymnasium and outdoor heated swimming pool. Our driver and guide for the week, Mike, drops the gear at the front door around 5.30pm. After a brief rest, we step into the heat and haze of Chiang Mai. The busy streets, the madness of the local markets and the appealing scents of the street cuisine fill my head with memories of my time in Bangkok only this year.

We all find culinary happiness at the Nang – Ceder Restaurant, prompting Mark and I to find the courage to ride a Tuktuk. The last time we attempted this feat was with Belinda Todd in the Bangkok show, and we have the bruises to prove it. We catch up with each other's lives over several bottles of wine and a garlic pepper and beef meal.

The bed is hard and small but forms a perfect cocoon as I sleep soundly until well after 10pm. Mark received word from the Thai Tourist Board last night that our Bangkok guide, Pop, will be in town next week which may give us the opportunity to catch up. He was a superb guy and looked after our every need. We owe him a visit.

A two-hour workout in the gymnasium this morning, which leaves me feeling refreshed, plus a quick dive into the heated pool are the only real highlights in this day off. Leanne Malcolm and husband Phil arrive at 3.00pm and entertain us with their travel horror stories. No matter how hard you try, it is still difficult to make this job easy. We go to a vegetarian restaurant around the corner from the hotel for a banquet of a meal – mainly chicken and rice.

Mark thinks that it may be a good idea to film some nightlife action. There's only one place to go for this. The night market sells a whole host of low price knick knacks (audio tapes for NZ$4, compact discs for NZ$12, laser pens for NZ$20) which are easily 'bartered' down by several 'baht'. The shopkeepers are all friendly and enthusiastic in their manner, and often refuse to let you pay the standard prices – not bargaining can be considered an insult. Tony is an absolute nightmare to shop with; his careful and efficient approach to purchasing causes me to lose patience. The boy's a nightmare, quite frankly. A few cheap audio tapes later, and I'm ready to retire.

Within 100 metres of the hotel entrance, a Thai gentleman thrusts a chalkboard in front of us. A simple message scrawled in bad, but legible handwriting:

'Everton vs Southampton. Live Tonight At 11.15pm.'

Given that we have lost touch with any sporting headlines or breaking news from home or abroad, this proves to be far too irresistible for us to miss. So Mark and I cheer in the new day watching the football in the English pub, The Bulldog, surrounded by Poms and Aussies. Familiar football chants echo down the heaving streets:

'You're not singing, you're not singing, you're singing anymore!'
'You're so shit it's unbelievable!'
'You're gonna cry in a minute, cry in a minute!'

Singing football songs in the middle of Asia.

It's almost unreal.

Everton lose.

They are so crap.

First day of shooting means a wake up call of 7.00am to capture the sunrise. My alarm clock has failed me again so I endeavour to make up lost time by skipping breakfast altogether.

It is marked with thick black ink at the top of my schedule that today is 'Temple Day' so Mike and his trusty band of supporters deliver us to Wat Chedi Luang. This particular temple was partially destroyed by earthquakes when still in its true magnificence. Attempts have been made to restore the old structure (evident in the newly cemented foundation stones) but controversy has raged within the local community as to whether the restoration is of any real benefit. Financially, it is something the locals are finding difficult to finance. Personally, the old ragged brick work adds to the Temple's mystique, while the recent additions contrast considerably. A series of majestic elephant statues guard the entrance while a string Buddha looks over the surrounding monasteries.

Wat Chiang Man provides a quieter, more reflective environment.

The temple is surrounded by resplendent stone statues of dragons and, you guessed it, elephants which were erected in a tribute to the role the animals play in transport, military and political purposes. There is a story surrounding a king, who sat atop one of his beasts during a violent storm and was killed by a thunderbolt from above.

Leanne delivers a small piece on the local lotus flower while I succumb to the charms of an elderly woman selling small baskets. On closer inspection I discover baby sparrows crawling helplessly around inside. She informs me that, with the purchase of a basket, I have the power to release the birds and bring good luck to my family. (Huh?) Feeling more sorry for the birds than desiring luck, I promptly make three purchases. The old woman has a nasty secret – she seems to have trained them to return once released and there is a line of chirping sparrows behind her on a hedge. My sparrows. The ones I help release. I think I can hear them laughing.

A quick visit to Wat U Mong before we all cry hungry and Mike delivers us to the nearby Custom Hotel for a smorgasbord. The selection of traditional Thai cuisine is vast, but the reliable favourite – rice and chicken – is still, nonetheless, the most popular.

It happens to be Tony's 30th birthday today – he's old now – so we make plans to celebrate tonight. Celebration plans are put on hold for a few hours while we venture uphill to the Wat Phra Dhut Doi Suthep – a magnificent temple positioned on the edge of a mountain range overlooking the city. The view of Chiang Mai is spectacular and Tony is delighted with the shots. Leanne and I ring the pilgrim bells and then finish our visit with a look inside the gold plated temple site.

Sadly, the whole area is swarming with tourists. The tranquil surroundings and mystical atmosphere are punctuated continuously with the gabble of tour guides, mechanical clicking of Polaroids and screams from visiting school groups. The only access from the road is an old rusty cable car, which scares Leanne into thinking we're all going to die. Judging by the way the machinery creaks and groans under our moderate weight, I fear that she could be right. To further intensify our annoyance at this rather unpleasant sight, several German tourists (in their haste to jump aboard the cable car) rudely barge their way onto our seats – we're still in them – and knock over some expensive camera gear. Several harsh words but no major incidents.

The heat has risen to 32°C even though we are now approaching almost 4.00pm. Mike predicts that tomorrow may be several degrees hotter and that the air-conditioning will need to be fixed. The trip downhill provides a cool refreshing breeze on our faces and, by the time we reach the bottom, we are dozing quietly. We meet for Tony's birthday meal.

At 9.15am Leanne and I assist an elderly lady to make umbrellas with paper and silk at Bor Sang Shelter Factory. The local markets are tourist-friendly; people are encouraged to be pro-active in the process of production. I have a multi-coloured tattoo put on my arm in print 'DPE Chiang Mai 1997' by an umbrella artist, which signals the end of our visit.

The woodwork factory is the next destination. My boredom is evident as we both stroll between the carvers and chisellers. One labourer is crouched over a pine table top chipping away at a complicated design. I endeavour to ease his pain with a back massage – his cries of 'enough, enough!' send me signals to stop. While Leanne is inspecting the crafted products, I pick up a nearby loudhailer:

'Thank you everybody for being such a great audience!'

No response.

'I've had a word with your boss and he wants you to have the day off.'

No response.

'OK, the whole week!'

No response.

The third factory visit is silverware, where I attempt to cook lunch of peppers and chilli for one of the saleswomen. She cooks Tony, Matt and myself a meal of rice and beef chilli for our effort in promoting her store. Their hospitality is quite astonishing, and we are ushered into their small office for our small banquet. As I devour the contents of my bowl, I notice that the room is covered in posters of Manchester United and Liverpool soccer players:

'Ohhh. Ryan Giggs. He is amazing!' I wonder if she is referring to his soccer skills.

'Maion' is a beautiful girl with a million dollar smile, which makes me wonder why she doesn't sell more stock, such is her exotic power. She finds it difficult to scrape together a living, and needs the security of a second occupation to live comfortably. Her work as a tour guide is helping to pay for a holiday abroad to visit her sister in Germany.

We drive into the Maesa Valley and towards the local orchid and butterfly farm for lunch. I let Mike do the ordering, which results in a spicy combination of chicken and prawn. Leanne has fish, which looks revolting. Our anguished cries of 'I don't see no ocean' discourage her from eating.

Snake Show. Plenty of lethal snakes in the form of python and cobra. The combination of professional handlers and secure cages make it perfectly safe. This isn't a display for the faint-hearted though. A couple sitting in front of us almost jump through the roof in response to the antics of the handlers – at one point they toss a 'snake-like' piece of rope into the crowd, scattering nervous tourists in all directions.

'God, I've had enough for today. Let's go home.'

Hooray for Mark.

An early start because we need to head north to Chiang Rai. Tang Dao Elephant Park was our first stop and we feed the animals. Bought feeding bananas for Baht 10.00 and then climb over a dodgy rope bridge to get to the Elephant show. Fed the baby elephants, bought a hat and went for 15 minute ride through the river and the jungle. Said farewell and climbed aboard the van.

A visit to the Chiang Dao caves which run under the Chiang Dao

---

Up the creek without a paddle, segment producer Mark Everton laughs nervously.

The DPE crew at the gates of narcotic central.

Mountain base. They are grotty and smelly. Tony reckons he's seen better in New Zealand. There is a local legend that says you must not remove anything from the caves or you will be doomed for life. Liking my head in its current position, I make a point of avoiding any small souvenirs. Despite the religious significance, the caves are unglamorous and tacky, the only thrill coming in the feeding of fish in a nearby estuary.

The remote Karen Village in Akha is a place to view the astonishing people of the 'Long Neck Tribe'. They adorn large brass rings around their necks – ranging from a couple for the junior associates, twenty for elder statesmen. Recent investigations have exposed a ring of tourist scams where youngsters are abducted from their native provinces and made to sell merchandise in villages such as this. Our wide-eyed fascination insures plenty of sales of garments and wallets.

One local tribesman tells us a story of one particular female member who made her way into the local town, against the wishes of the tribe elders. This resulted in a permanent confiscation of her neckrings and, due to the deterioration of her neck muscles, she was unable to hold her head in an upright position. She was well hidden from the cameras.

Leanne and I muck up several takes of an item proving how tired we are. A two hour drive to Chiang Rai – a beautiful island hotel – time for a quick workout in the gym and then dinner.

A sleep-in followed by a lovely breakfast – buffet style. Straight onto the Mekong River – the site of plenty of opium dealing (legal) and longtail boats. The Golden Triangle is one of the most photographed places in the world and we take time to climb onto the viewing platform to overlook the three countries – Laos, Burma and Thailand. The boats are thin but extremely fast so the noise can be heard for miles around. The journey back is long and boring but there's plenty of entertainment in the form of walkman and tapes.

We travel for an hour just to get back to Chiang Rai – It takes another three and a half excruciating hours before we reach Chiang Mai. The majority of the journey is taken on rough, poorly lit and dangerous roads so to reach our destination without major incident is a credit to our driver. And to God.

The energy-sapping journey last night means that we arrived at a ridiculous hour of the morning and therefore sleep in until around 12.00pm. On waking, I have a quick bite to eat before hitting the local markets. My collection of audio tapes continues to grow – almost out of control – so I ask Tony to forcibly remove me should my purchasing turn serious. I'm sorry but $3 per cassette is such a steal.

A stall selling sunglasses is manned by an absolute beauty, who is snottier than Hilda Ogden. I try some charm but it's wasted on her scowling mug. I'm in the process of giving up when Mark hires a Tuktuk for our 'piece de resistance' opening shot. Tony attaches the Triple 9 camera to the top of the van and we proceed to drive through the inner city streets. Van following Tuktuk. The result is a brisk and bustling shot of the two presenters turning pale with the fear of nearly crashing. Mark is pleased.

Due to the countless occasions on which I have had to hustle my way to a bargain, I am often given the task of purchasing goods for the team. This evening Mark and Tony want a sports bag each, so I insist on keeping the cameras rolling for the whole sequence. Risking embarrassment, most shopkeepers refuse filming permission, so the cameras are in hidden positions.

I start my attack:

'Evening.'

'Hello mister. Good bargain, good bargain for you.'

'The purple sports bag up there. How much?'

'800 baht. Very good quality, you want look?'

She gets the bag down. In these situations you must look as disinterested as possible. I poke fun at the fact that the bag is an odd colour, and that it is flimsy and badly sewn. There is a simple rule to follow when bargaining: Never, ever verbally quote a price. Once you've mentioned a figure, they'll never drop below it.

'Ok, what about a discount for me?'

She smiles. Although she's young, she looks to be a tough player.

'Discount for you mister. 500.'

'Nope. Lower.'

'OK mister, 450 baht?'

I grab the calculator and type in 400, careful not to drop the price too quickly.

'No way, mister. No way.'

'I want to buy two.'

'Oh.'

I grab the calculator again and type in 350.

'I'll buy two for that amount.'

'Please mister. More baht, more baht.'

'This isn't a bloody charity love. Two bags or I'm walking.'

I start walking. I must sound like a real wanker, but the negotiation is an important challenge, and you need to be tough. Shop owners and vendors will quite happily rip you off given half the chance.

'Please mister. More baht, more baht.'

'Bye.'

'OK. 350 baht.'

She trudges off to the storeroom, a broken woman.

Mark and Tony get their bags. We get the footage. Phil has chosen a

NIGHTLINE presenter Leanne Malcolm.

delightful Thai restaurant to in which to finish the day. A bottle of water has leaked all over my diaries tonight, so I attempt a quick patch-up job before retiring. Have to make today's notes on a bunch of restaurant napkins. No expense spared.

Few and far between. I'm referring to the number of full rest days we've had simply to unwind and relax during the last six months of shooting this show. Mark has left a note under my door this morning:

'No shooting needed this morning. Meet out front at 5.00pm for game of Takraw.'

The others are taking advantage of their allocated rest by sleeping in. I make it to the gym but can only muster up a half-hearted effort. I retire to bed and sleep for an additional few hours. The day is muggy and hot, which prompts a late afternoon swim for everybody. There is also a few hours for us to shop for various items. Tony has purchased almost 12 laser pointers, I have finished up with countless audio tapes. Thank goodness we're only staying for a week – any longer and I'd be skint to my teeth.

The final commitment for our Chiang Mai shoot is a game of Takraw with Mike and his team. Takraw is a form of volleyball with several notable differences:

1. The ball is made of several intertwined bands of plastic.
2. There are three players per side.
3. The game is played on concrete.
4. You can play the ball with any part of your body, except the hands or arms.
5. Three touches to get the ball back over the net.
6. If you are an ex-rugby player, have the flexibility of a brick and the hand-eye co-ordination of a dead wildebeast, this really isn't your game.

The players are very accommodating to my lack of Tackraw ability, which slows the game but heightens the comic factor. All 5 players are incredibly flexible and possess such an array of shots that almost defy their stocky stature. One particular player – name not given – is a short, squat fatboy, who proceeds to perform gravity-defying leaps and kicks that would even shadow the skills of Mary Lou Retton. We are very grateful for their time and patience, and I depart with body intact but sporting reputation in shatters.

That, officially, is that. The camera is switched off in anticipation of a long journey home. The night, however, is still young. Mark needs to get make some phone calls so Matt, Tony and myself go in search of a traditional Thai massage. There are plenty of different clinics available and we decide on the suspiciously named 'Feel Good Shop'. A traditional massage will cost the equivalent of NZ$8 for two hours but its no easy ride. The idea of a petite Asian woman manipulating and contorting your body into every possible position is exciting but scary at the same time.

After two hours of squeezing, probing, rubbing and, oh yes, massage, we are on our way. A quiet late evening meal in Pizza Hut brings the day to a close.

We were supposed to meet up with our Bangkok guide Pop but communication breakdown has prevented our meeting. To come this far around the world and not meet up is a shame but he could well be on his way home by now. We leave a message at the front desk and hope he receives it.

The journey home will take us from Chiang Mai to Bangkok to Hong Kong to Auckland. We anticipate a pleasant journey, and have the joy of accompanying some American tourists on the trip. I sit next to Vern Lutz, from Texas. His breath smells but he's interesting to talk to.

Chapter 15 | Dubai, United Arab Emirates

Day 103, Tuesday 25th November

Sad news for Nick Eynon today. An early morning phone call reveals that a good friend has been killed in Britain – prompting a rush of desperate calls to friends positioned in every corner of the globe. It has knocked my priorities into shape and suddenly Hong Kong becomes a very long way from anywhere. I feel lonely.

I have often contemplated the likely events should a loved one die when I was based overseas, and now it seems my energies are directed to attending the funeral – to be held in England on Monday. Travel is in limbo – my mind is racing at a million miles an hour.

What takes priority in a situation like this?

Will it be too expensive or impractical to fly out to Britain?

We catch the flight out and arrive in Bahrain 9 hours later and then trip another hour to Dubai. We pull up to the Metropolitan Palace Hotel where Rob McLaughlin (Director) and Jude Callen (Researcher) also arrive from a night out. Rob is in good spirits and can't stop talking up the luxuries of the Middle East. I sit down and talk over the possibility of flying out for the funeral with Rob and despite the awkward logistics, it will be feasible.

Is it practical? Probably not.

'We have about 2 free days in which to rest at the conclusion of the shoot so we could always make up for lost time there.'

I can tell that Rob doesn't want me to go. There has been too much work done in preparation for me to throw a spanner in the works. Our shooting schedule is tight enough without the worry of re-arranging everything. I'll give it 24 hours before I reply.

Petra Bagust, my co-presenter for this show, settles into her hotel room with plenty of ease. I have long wanted to work with her, so it should be fun for two young presenters to let their hair down.

No sleep but took some time to get onto the roof and enjoy the fantastic view from the comfort of a rooftop swimming pool. I relax in a deck chair for a few sun-drenched hours and end up tanning my ailing body.

The hotel, aptly named the Metropolitan Palace, is the most expensive and well kept that we have encountered on our travels. Miniature waterfalls and fountains highlight the marble-floored interior. Two glass elevators whisk guests from their rooms to the dining room, breakfast parlour, massage unit, outdoor swimming pool and multi-use gymnasium. The concierge informs me that it was only opened a month ago, so we are privileged to be early pioneers of the 'Met'. Room service is swift and immaculately presented on a fully mounted trolley – they bring your meals to any part of the hotel, even if you are poolside.

There is an outing planned for this afternoon, but I am lacking so much sleep that I choose to stay. Tony isn't feeling 100% so we both decide to watch a bit of television and settle down with some Soy Ginger Chicken and Fruit Platter – delivered straight to the door.

I end up crashing out until 8.00pm. I drift in and out of sleep.

The temperature outside is pleasant enough, the air-conditioning hums vigilantly in my room providing a comfortable environment in which to sleep. Sadly, I find it difficult. I call the United Kingdom to try and organise flights. It seems that I will have no trouble flying into Britain, but coming out of Heathrow (especially around this peak season for travelling) will be difficult. The costs range from NZ$1,200 to NZ$2,000 which will take me from Dubai to Rome to London.

I give it plenty of thought before leaving a message on Rob's answer machine:

'Yeah, it's Nick. Flying out is going to be too much of a pain in the arse. I'll stay.'

After making the decision, I sleep easier.

We meet at 8.00am but I have already been awake for several hours. Zaric and Mike are our drivers this morning and their four-wheel drives take us towards the desert. The landscape is, quite frankly, bewildering. Miles upon miles of golden sand fills the entire horizon and the glare prompts swift use of every pair of sunglasses.

An hour south of the city we pull into a roadside oasis to find our falconry display team. The sole human element takes the form of a Belgian expatriate called Dan. The rest of his squad come with wings: a

NICK, DAN AND TIGER.

falcon called Tess, a baby eagle called Marvin and a fighting hawk named Tiger. After various manoeuvres, Dan lets Petra and I perform a number of flying stunts including a fly'n'fetch with Tiger. Dan explains that many trained birds still hunt in the wild for live prey and he has recently lost two birds. He suspects that they were killed by other trained falcons.

We hit the dunes! Mike revs the jeep through the sand with considerable expertise. Sadly, Zaric has been too adventurous and ends up getting stuck. We spend a half an hour digging the front axle free from the sand until a good push encourages the buggy to roll on. Zaric is bemused: 'This is the first time I have ever been stuck!' he seems downtrodden.

Next it is time to surf the sand, Mike is an able snowboarder but it takes me four attempts before I get down the dune in one piece. Mike holds the national record for speed skiing on the sand so I'm in esteemed company. The weather conditions have caused my hair to transform from jet-black to golden brown. The sand will take ages to wash out.

We jump into the van and make our way through Oman to do some wadi-bashing. This involves Petra and Mike negotiating several riverbeds at high speed in the four-wheel drive. We stop for lunch at a poolside lodge before grinding our way through several more miles of stony riverbeds. The darkness falls quickly and we have to abandon the rest of the shoot. We have captured all that we needed today anyway.

We finish the day at a traditional Arab Camp where belly dancing, smoking hubbly-bubbly and tattoo painting are some the activities on offer. Petra gets a tattoo, while I join a couple of elderly Arab gentlemen for a smoke of their herb-pipe. The hubbly-bubbly tastes and smells of peaches, so it turns into a rather pleasant experience. Thankfully, the after effects will not be as lasting as Petra's tattoo which will not fade for at least 15 days.

We make a hasty return to the hotel and a quick visit to the gym for the whole crew before we crash.

Another early start and camel racing is the first visit this morning.

DESTINATION ANYWHERE

Tales of the Arabian Days, guest presenter Petra Bagust of Ice-TV is kneeling at left.

Sadly the authorities are reluctant to let us into the racecourse with our camera gear. Being refused permission comes as no real surprise after the stories that Mike has told us. It has something to do with a recent visit by an overseas film crew that exposed a ring of child abduction – children as young as four years being smuggled from Pakistan and India to be used as camel jockeys.

We decide that the racing can wait and venture onward to the Sheik's very own camel stud farm. On the way, I throw up outside the van. The lack of sleep has caused my body to shout 'Excuse me, but give me a break!'

We feed and play with the camels before Rob requests a toilet stop that lasts about 15 minutes. He has an upset stomach and Tim is feeling light-headed so we must look like a bunch of hospital patients. I talk to Rob about the fact that Tony and Tim are knackered and need a couple of hours of rest. It is decided that we should abandon the morning's shoot in favour of time off by the pool. Things have been stressed recently and the rest gives everybody an extra burst.

We meet again at 3.30pm and film some montage collections and then onto Sheik Mohammed's house where we are met by an Arab aristocrat, and friend to the Bagusts' called Boukhit. He presents me with a tailored Arab robe and head dress and details the various intricacies of traditional Arab dress – even though females seem to be more affected by the strict rules. Outside the house a bunch of local youths clown around playing a game of cricket, I join in and hit a six – followed by my bails getting smashed by the next ball.

Onto the gold souk, where we experience similar crowd problems to those when we were in India. The camera attracts plenty of attention, and within seconds we are surrounded by curious onlookers – not waving, not skylarking – just standing there observing. I attempt to divert attention by singing *New York, New York* to the masses. This presents Rob with the opportunity to film the piece with Petra without any spectators. I feel like a complete idiot when someone requests an Arabic tune.

Petra buys some gold while a group of locals quiz me as to why we're not going to Egypt. I explain that the recent violence in Cairo does not encourage tourism. The local group does not seem deterred:

'Yes, there are plenty of murders. But the dead are only Westerners.'

Can I go now?

It's a midday start the following day. The schedule reads:

11.00am   *Lunch at Hotel Breakfast Parlour*
11.30am   *Pack gear and meet Mike at Metropolitan Palace entrance*
12.00pm   *Depart for Jeremiah Beach Resort*
                 PTC on the wharf – travel tip
                 PTC on the beach – walking naked
                 PTC – the most amazing resort in the world!

We are told that Jeremiah Beach is one of the best resorts in the world – and only a 20-minute drive away – so we jump into the four-wheel drive, eager with anticipation. We are not disappointed. The beach resort complex comes complete with three outdoor heated pools, volleyball courts, indoor sports arena, four fully catered restaurants and extensive recreational facilities. When fully completed, the Jeremiah Beach Hotel will be the tallest hotel in the world – the staggering structure reminds us of the space shuttle launch pad at Cape Canaveral. Wandering on the beach, feeling the golden sand between my toes, it's a shame we can't stay for a casual swim.

Our return to the city is met by scenes of celebration and jubilation. Inner-city traffic jams, flag waving and tooting horns signify a football win to the Iranian National Soccer Team. News has just been received that they have unexpectedly triumphed over Australia, sending the Middle East team to the World Cup finals next year.

'We are so happy' screams one man 'Now people can take Iran seriously as a football nation'. I'd take Iran pretty seriously for anything.

Another monster workout this morning. The gymnasium is a superb facility and it has been an added advantage having personal trainers on standby, to assist you with your weights programme.

More sport is planned for this morning at the Emirate Golf Club, frequently listed as one of the best golf courses in the world. Every year it hosts the PGA Classic – a highly respected and financially lucrative tournament attracting a large number of esteemed professionals. The resident curator meets us on the 14th hole. Shaun is an Australian super-intendent who is employed to keep the greens, well, as green as possible. Not an easy job in the Middle East.

As well as supervising the general maintenance of the course (he reveals that they pump 1.3 million gallons of water everyday in order to keep it green and lush) he must find time to play the holes to ensure correct grass length and run speed. To fit into his schedule, it is decided that our interview will be conducted while playing a few holes.

Carole Read, the marketing director, issues a couple of golf carts and the Kiwi crew are let loose on the Emirates Golf Course. I line up at the 14th tee, having never used a wooden driver before and start proceedings. My lack of golfing co-ordination becomes obvious with my first ground stroke. The clump of turf almost wallops my host in the eye. We disperse to the next hole:

'You must be pretty well looked after,' I throw the inevitable curveball.

'You wanna know the truth?' he whispers, 'I make so much money, I don't know what to do with it. It's because I have minimal overheads. Company car, insurance, accommodation, medical – it's all supplied by the club.'

'What about green fees?'

'Paid for.'

'Flights?'

'Paid for.'

'Food?'

'Paid for.'

'What the hell do you pay for?'

'Now you're getting personal!'

Greg Norman and Seve Ballesteros are regular competitors at the course and Shaun takes plenty of pride in an occupation that enables him to mix with such prestigious golfing talent. The carts wind in and out of the dunes and, inevitably, Shaun is called away to activate the sprinkler system – which must be engaged at least four times a day under his supervision. We complete the shoot and then muscle our way onto the driving range. We treat ourselves to a few buckets of practice balls.

Petra and Judy have taken time to shop with their new found friend who clearly enjoys spoiling his two Western friends. We all meet at the docks around 5.00pm for a boat trip down the Creek. The lights of the high-rise buildings illuminate the city as the sun disappears below the cloudless horizon.

There is plenty of excitement in the crew as the aim of this morning's schedule is to purchase Turkish carpets in Al Sharjah. Because I am not required for the shoot, I decide to wander the streets in search of some bargain items. Because I haven't even opened my wallet on this trip, I have the luxury of some extra cash to spend.

The local shopping centre offers plenty of electronics and computer gadgetry, but my interest is in the sports clothing. Nike, Reebok, Adidas and Puma are all well represented, and the prices vary according to whether you are buying from a mainstream distributor or dodgy back-street dealer.

The crew return from Sharjah at 4.00pm which gives everybody the chance to quickly spruce up and get their boogie shoes on. The outing tonight promises to be an outstanding evening of dance/techno wizardry in the form of British-run 'Ministry of Sound'. Held at the local DIMC nightclub, 'Ministry' attracts thousands of clubbers (largely expatriate British) who gather to celebrate the latest in global dance themes. Such is the popularity of this event, British-based DJ's are flown out for the occasion:

'Everybody in the house, say yeah!'

'Is there anyone from Birmingham here tonight?'

'We'd like to welcome the film crew from Noo Zeelind.'

The sweaty security guards are having problems with the swelling crowd outside. There is no confrontational feeling, only keen punters who are waiting for their money's worth – about NZ$30 for a ticket. Several 'ravers' are queuing in typical attire: roadwork tops, bare chests and whistles – a sight so common outside any British nightclub. As our liaison officer declares:

'This is just a little piece of England in the middle of the desert.'

'Any famous acts that have appeared?'

'A few years ago we had Boy George. Last year Neil Tennant from the Pet Shop Boys turned up. And there are rumours that Aqua will be here tonight.'

'Will they have to pay to get in?'

'Of course.'

We wrap up the night around 3.00am. Much too late for Tony and Tim to be working. No chance for a dance – too much gear to look after. Mike is determined to keep partying until the early morning, but we politely decline!

Nothing to report this morning. For the first time since I've started writing these diaries, I am almost stuck for words.

I had problems last night with my facsimile. When the crew want to make calls to New Zealand from overseas, we are lucky enough to be given Telecom Calling Cards to enable an easy passage of communication to loved ones and family. The 'primary' 0800 number is dialled (connects you with a Telecom operator), followed by your password and then the desired connection. Sadly, there is no 0800 number for the United Arab Emirates, and all calls must be made directly from the hotel rooms.

Last night I made a 20 minute call, and it will cost me NZ$175.

The day has been set aside for picking up general views of the city.

With nothing to write, I'm signing off.

I have sore arms from another intense workout. Efrin is trying to kill me for sure. Despite the huge amount of pain and anguish he is putting me through, there is a notable growth in my biceps and triceps this week. Even though he is paid for supervision, I have bought him a cassette tape, 'LL Cool J's Greatest Hits', for his efforts.

Filming is completed this morning on the roof of the hotel (another travel tip) and Rob proposes a quick game of golf at the International Golf Arena to fill the time until lunch. We are given free use of the Short-Nine course and a fun-filled three hours of friendly golf commences. Sadly, the competitive juices are flowing in abundance from the moment the first ball is struck, and the 'fun' is fast removed from a pressure-cooker nine holes of fiercely rivalled golf.

Rob loses a ball on the 7th, and misses a 'sitter' putt on the 8th prompting a thrown club. I laugh so hysterically the tears are streaming down my face. Tony is losing his rhythm and, following a promising start, has disappeared down the order by the 5th. Tim is playing his first ever game of golf and despite digging up half the desert in an effort to make contact with the ball, he is the fastest learner I have ever played with.

'FORE!'

'Four what?'

'Don't worry.'

The competition becomes a two-horse race between Mike 'I swear I've only played a couple of times' Smith and Nick 'brilliant and crap at the same time' Eynon.

In the end, Mike is the more consistent and beats me to the finish post by a couple of strokes. The morning has been thoroughly enjoyable, and the tensions of an overseas shoot have disappeared completely. The temperature has soared well into the thirties, but it is a pleasant dry heat.

I've decided to spend the rest of the day by the swimming pool, and the lads decide to do the same. Petra and her mum are departing tonight for Phuket as an extension of their Middle East holiday so they pack and then head to the airport.

The airport is a mass of smelly, sweaty people. It brings back frightening memories of our airport dilemma in Delhi. Monstrous queues for the baggage x-ray machine twist their way down the departure terminal. Because of customs commitments, Tony disappears for an hour to ensure our equipment's safe passage.

Almost 90% of today's travellers seem to be heading to Pakistan or India, so there is a positive feeling within the crew that our flight won't be overbooked. Rob has managed to pack his carpets into Tony's tripod case, so the gear is significantly heavier leaving than it was arriving.

An hour later, we haven't moved from our position in the queue. Last.

Our sanity is saved by a vigilant liaison officer who whisks us to the front of the business section, checks our luggage through to Auckland, and then issues some lounge passes. All in the space of 20 minutes. We appreciate his goodwill, and return the compliment by discussing the fortunes of the New Zealand cricket team. He is a fanatic, and surprises me with his in-depth knowledge of the sport:

'The Kiwis were really robbed in the last world cup. That game in Napier was a very good game, very good game. Then we were lucky to beat you in the semi-final.'

He is referring to Pakistan's defeat of the Black Caps in the 1992 Cricket World Cup.

'You know, the whole of Pakistan thought New Zealand were the best team in the world at that time.' he declares.

'Well, we're struggling a bit now.' I add

'Yes. Yes. Now New Zealand is truly awful.'

We wait for 20 minutes before we are summoned to the aircraft. The familiar smells and sounds of the Cathay Pacific 747 fills our nostrils, the customary orange juice and hot towels are distributed and *South China Morning Post* is handed around. Luckily enough, we have been allocated 'bubble' seats (on the upstairs level of the plane) and there is much relief when the plane taxis towards the runway.

Our first meal will be a light lunch consisting of a full salad, choice of breads, fish platter, beef and rice, fruit plate and various cheeses. The menus are handed out, and then the flight commander asks for seat belts to be fastened.

The Middle East disappears beneath heavy cloud as we fly north to Bahrain. The coarse, weather-beaten sands of the United Arab Emirates grow steadily smaller through my viewing window.

We leave behind a truly beautiful country.

PICTURES THAT TELL A STORY

Faces and places not yet chronicled

Nick's graffiti tribute to U2, at the Wharfside
Warehouse in Dublin where the band held their
first-ever rehearsals. Guest presenter Theresa
Healey is at left in the photo above.

An Irish roadsign demonstrating the dangers
of falling to stop.

Kerre Woodham goes British.

Rome is where the heart is.

Chapter 16 | ZIMBABWE

Day 113, Friday 12th December

Auckland delivers a magnificent afternoon of sunshine as we rally for trolleys outside the International terminal. The check-in procedure has become so routine we could probably do it in our sleep. Everything runs smoothly, our burdensome collection of luggage has been registered and stored, and at 1.15pm we board our plane.

Tim and Tony, my only two travel companions for this journey, make hasty last minute phone calls to loved ones while my major concern lies solely in the in-flight movie. Oh, goody! *Independence Day!* Again.

Nigel Carpenter (director) and Jude Callen (researcher) are waiting for us in Zimbabwe while my co-presenter Theresa Healey (Carmen on *Shortland Street*) is travelling from Sydney. The business class section is fairly quiet, until three hours out of Auckland, when a young infant starts to scream uncontrollably. I turn my walkman up really loud.

Hong Kong is visited, Theresa is collected, we get Business Class to Johannesburg, but have to endure a five-hour wait in the lounge of South African Airways. Due to the domestic connection, there was no organised hospitality available. A fair amount of pleading is required to convince the stewardess that we need a place to rest. Poor Tony has to transport his 12.5 kilogram camera everywhere we go, so there are muffled cheers when the South African Airways representative says:

'Will, wee dornt do thees sort of theeng too effurry win.'

(Well, we don't do this sort of thing for everyone)

Typical South African hospitality. Firm but fair.

Worrying reports have seeped through to us that the phone/fax system in Zimbabwe is not operational due to the heavy rainfall. The communication strike rate in Africa is typical of any Third World continent: if it works, you're lucky. We have been advised to call any important numbers at home from Jo'burg while we have the chance. It may be several days, or weeks, before lines in Zimbabwe are restored.

The landscape suddenly transforms into a flat expanse of sun-drenched trees and clay coloured soil, punctuated occasionally with small outback settlements – the only real indication of civilisation. My Casio G-Shock chimes at midday, just as we arrive into the sweltering heat of Victoria Falls. A familiar figure emerges on the tarmac as we struggle our way through the tropical conditions toward the terminal. Nigel cheerfully greets us with his typical enthusiasm, but explains that several problems have arisen.

'I've just returned from Harare,' he explains 'to collect a representative from the Tourist Board, fly him out here just so that he can sign your immigration forms.'

His frustration is evident, and further compounded when our luggage is refused entry. Our passports and visas have been processed correctly, but the 12 cases of television equipment prove to be too much of a major issue for the customs officers. The carney we carry (the official document shown to customs) does not list Zimbabwe as a legitimate port-of-call, which prompts the host officials to decline entry for the gear. After travelling non-stop for three days, this is about as welcome as paparazzi at a Royal barbie. The temperature rises within the corrugated-iron walls of the Arrivals Terminal and Nigel finally decides to call a quick huddle:

'What the hell are we going to do if they won't let us in?' I ask.

'Get in the plane and go home, I s'pose,' Nigel replies.

'How about a free bloody holiday?' someone suggests.

It is decided that the crew should head to the hotel while our director remains at the airport to sort out 'our little diplomatic incident'. The tremendous disorganisation of the authorities has produced two immediate options: we can buy our way into the country (perhaps this should read 'bribe') by paying ZM$500,000 or returning to NZ the next day.

Our driver transports us to the welcome reclines of Masuwe Lodge – an open camp accommodation centre which is positioned in the middle of a nature park, enabling the wildlife to roam free between rooms. The Lodge has a swimming pool, dining room area and 10 huts which can accommodate up to twenty people at one time. The US$250-per-night package includes all food, drink and safari activity – considerably expensive, but the best way of viewing game and living comfortably while on holiday in a safari environment.

There is nothing to do but wait, sitting in the pool and drinking gallons of water and orange juice, before a phone call from the airport (four hours after we set foot in Victoria Falls) assures us that the gear has been cleared through customs and will be due back at the camp soon. The tepid sun sets the early evening clouds alight, as we rest on our deck chairs weary from travel, but content in the knowledge that we will be able to proceed as planned.

No surprise when Nigel declares the day as a no-go for shooting. We had planned to visit a nearby crocodile park and traditional dance performance but the day has sluggishly crept into night and, with the aroma of Rhodesian cooking filling our nostrils, it prompts an evening of chat and laughter with our two hosts Martin and Phillipa.

I giggle at the bedtime instructions given before we venture back to our huts:

'Make sure you keep to the paths when you return to your bed. People have been eaten.'

I also take the precaution of spraying the hut before lowering the mossie nets in order to prevent any malaria-carrying little bugger from sucking on my ankles all evening. The sound of the bush sends me to sleep, although 36 hours of jetlag help the cause.

I have several mosquito signatures on my lower leg this morning – somewhat baffling, as I have taken every possible precaution – but I have contributed to their discolouration by itching continuously during breakfast.

There is no lack of meat in this country. Every meal served has some form of springbok, beef, lamb or pork supplied – no doubt contributing to the big-boned nature of the local whites – and breakfast doesn't disappoint. A huge pot of bacon and eggs is served and gratefully demolished. We compare stories of our first night 'outback'. Tim hasn't slept, Theresa woke far too early and I am covered in bites.

Nigel has aptly labelled this as 'Hell Day' in reference to the huge amount of work we must get through in order to make up for lost time yesterday. We begin early and make the 30 minute trip to the airport to film aerial shots. We anticipate similar red-tape difficulties that were encountered yesterday with the airport officials but there is another worry.

A convoy of 20 armoured vehicles sit in formation on the runway and

Martin reveals that the US Secretary of State (and reputedly the world's most powerful woman) Madeleine Albright arrives this morning for a four-day holiday. Security insists that we spend minimal time on the tarmac, so we end up making several trips on and off the runway, setting up gear. The first activity is an ultralight flight, and our English expatriate pilot Dave sets the morning in motion when he lifts the landing gear off *terra firma*.

For the flight, I am holding the digital camera between my legs and Tony has strapped the Triple 9 Pencil Cam to the wing so every possible camera angle seems to be covered. The trip lasts 35 minutes and takes in the magnificence of Victoria Falls. We are unable to fly too close to the thundering wall of water – due to the powerful thermals that can easily throw the ultra-light into a dangerous spin. Dave flies us over Masuwe Lodge but Theresa is still in bed. No real chance of finding out whether or not she has a bald spot.

The action is almost over in the blink of an eye. On our return we discover that Madeleine hasn't arrived so Tony swaps places and Dave does another circuit with the trained professional next to him. There are a number of American agents hanging around trying desperately hard to blend in; with their perfectly ironed khaki pants, crew cuts and spotless trainers, they stick out like sore thumbs.

The staff at Masuwe Lodge have kept some lunch in the oven, (it is almost 10.30am) which is happily devoured in minutes. Theresa introduces us to Trevor Soma, our guide for Victoria Falls, a large half-caste Zimbabwean who seems to light up the room with his immense personality. We all warm to his sense of humour, and he strikes up an immediate rapport with the crew. Trevor works as the Public Relations Manager for 'Shearwater Adventure Holidays' and is in charge of the rafting programme for the Zambesi River – the ideal person to have in charge of proceedings.

'Hey, Nick. You're brown, I'm brown. We could be brothers!' he roars.

Trevor takes us to visit his apartment block – a collection of units hosting rafting and canoeing instructors from all corners of the globe – and we thoroughly investigate the premises. After completely excavating the contents of his closet (I had a peak in his fridge! Full of meat!) we head downtown. Trevor seems to know everybody in town (not hard when there are only a few thousand permanent residents!) and our journey is interrupted with various cries of welcome from passing citizens:

'Hey, Soma! Whadssup?'

'Trev man, what's the vibe, buddy?'

The heat is bearable at this stage of the year but Trevor explains that the temperature can rise to well over 45°C in the heart of the summer. Considering we have been in the sunlight for nearly 7 hours already, we are grateful that the sun is not too punishing. Downtown Victoria Falls is no staggering metropolis, the stagnant flow of traffic deprives the town of traffic lights or pedestrian crossings, and you could probably sleep on the pavement during rush-hour and not even stir.

Trevor explains that the town's enduring existence is due solely to the seventh 'Natural Wonder of the World' that is Victoria Falls – aptly named by locals as 'the smoke that thunders' it was the discovery of explorer David Livingstone (of 'Doctor Livingstone I presume?' fame) who became the first white man to uncover the colossal wall of water in 1856. He presumptuously named the falls after his Queen. The mighty Zambesi River provides up to 500,000 cubic litres of water per minute that flows over the kilometre-wide Falls, before it plunges into the Bakota Gorge below. This mammoth amount – a total that increases ten-fold during the height of wet season – forms the single largest curtain of water in the world.

The Zambesi itself is the fourth largest river in Africa. It flows for about 2700 kilometres from its source in northern Zambia, and the 'Destination Planet Earth' crew will be formally introduced tomorrow when Trevor takes us white-water rafting. An activity, he promises, that will change our lives forever.

Our visit to a nearby Crocodile Farm provides some hands-on, pro-active activity with crocodile and lion cub feeding. This establishment serves a dual purpose – to restock the badly depleted river and to rear crocs for their valuable skin. Every year approximately 2500 eggs are collected, hatched, reared and then returned into the wild to provide a safer percentage of surviving infants.

Theresa is not keen enough to get into the cage with the animals but I fake bravery and feed the lions by the hand. We also handle a couple of baby crocodiles, with the help of a gamekeeper. Despite their infancy, the reptiles are aggressive and unforgiving in appearance.

'Those crocs you handled are about 3 years old,' Trevor whispers in my ear.

I give him a quizzical look. 'The gamekeeper told me they were only babies?'

Trevor explains that the stress of being handled everyday (something that crocodiles don't encounter in the wild) has stunted their growth considerably. Despite their ruthless, ferocious and barbarous persona, I feel sorry for the young gators. Some additional action is provided in the wildlife section, when a gazelle and a lion cub are accidentally shepherded into the same cage. Due to the lack of hunting experience and its tame upbringing, there is no ruthless slaughter of the smaller animal by the cub – much to our disappointment. It simply roars then falls asleep. Useless bugger.

The temperature is slowly bronzing my olive skin, and the heat is steadily sapping the energy from the crew. Theresa does a 'drinks run' and we have a quick breather in the van before moving on.

The helicopter ride over the Falls that was planned for this morning has been conveniently re-scheduled for this afternoon and Theresa has the pleasure of flying in the front seat. For filming purposes, Tim and Nigel are squashed into the back while Tony, not for the first time I might add, hangs out the window – held only by the cords of a safety harness. Trevor and I are disappointed that we can't go up for the ride but are adequately compensated when Nigel suggests that we take a shot of the chopper lifting off – from underneath the belly of the vehicle.

At first I thought he was joking, but when the pilot nods in agreement I realise that there is no turning back. Trevor and I are almost lifted off the ground with the backdraft power of the rotors, and I manage to get some great shots of the lift-off as the pilot hovers a few metres over us and then peels away.

The final stop for the day is the main attraction for this little town in the northwest corner of the country. Trevor admits that the town of Victoria Falls is unashamedly geared to tourism, providing daily trips to every possible outdoor activity site in close proximity. When it comes to viewing the falls they encourage groups to visit during the dry season as, throughout the wet season, the heavy volume of water creates a cloudy mist of water vapour, which shrouds the view. We seem to have come at the right time.

'You can hear the roar from miles away!' Theresa screams.

The noise is incredible and Tim is hearing it all in pristine stereo sound through his equipment. The breathtaking view proves to be the ideal way of finishing the day.

The trip back to Masuwe Lodge is spent sleeping and we struggle to make conversation over the table as our eyelids get heavier. More meat for dinner, plus a visit from a herd of elephants at the Lodge waterhole. Theresa sees the bull elephant's penis but no one is around to share the joy of her discovery. Finally, after two days of valiant effort, Tony and I are able to make contact with home even though Martin explains that the phone lines will only be operational for a few hours so we should make the most of it.

Only a few hours slumber. The wildlife was quiet outside my hut, so lack of sleep was self-induced. Theresa and I both wake at the same time and discuss politics over our balconies. Unfortunately, we fail to realise the other huts are in such close proximity and are soundly threatened at breakfast to shut up. It's another early call for a day of adventure and we meet at the Cattleman's Restaurant with a collection of Australian, South African and Zimbabwean adventure holiday makers for the Shearwater Rafting Experience.

Trevor explains the nitty gritty of the rafting course to the 180 punters who have paid good money to get thrown down the furious Zambesi River. Trevor's speech is very entertaining and several nervous faces are relieved of their tension through his antics. The overriding theme is enjoyment but the safety factor is also emphasised. Rafting down the Zambesi started in the 1980's and offers some of the world's wildest white water. This stretch of the River rates a 5 (white water runs are graded 1 to 6 in difficulty) while the Falls themselves are a 6 – unrunnable! Despite its size, it is a relatively safe river to raft – it's warm so there's no risk of hypothermia, and very deep which eliminates the danger of hitting rocks. Trevor is proud of his company's track record:

'We have never, ever lost any souls overboard,' he smiles, 'the only company with a 100% track record you know.'

A slow and often slippery trek to the River before we set up cameras and sound equipment on the raft. Threats of hippos and crocs do not discourage us from jumping in the water to cool off before we 'lock and load'. The first 5 rapids are tame but then things get really hairy. Trevor is on board to help, but our instructor Hippo has things under control as we race down some perilous waterways. On reaching Rapid Number 10

(Gnashing Jaws of Death), we are given the choice of 2 channels – left or right, dangerous or safe. Trevor and Hippo explain that if one single person is unhappy about the dangerous route then we don't go. A French tourist called Angelique refuses to go down so Tony and I have to hitch a ride with a separate raft.

Our daredevil approach is rewarded. We are both flung out of the boat by the tremendous force of the rapid, much to the delight of our fellow crew members. I manage to hold on to the guide rope of my raft – but am still thrown about like a stray sock in a washing machine. We look bedraggled and sore but the camera has captured the all the action. Our raft turns into a floating ambulance as we end up rescuing a truckload of people who are thrown off their rafts – testament to the ferocious power of the Zambesi. A few fearful looks but no injuries and only damaged egos need repair. Lunch is provided at the end of the first 11 rapids, and the meal of chicken sandwiches is quickly devoured. Due to our tough scheduling, we are unable to complete a full day's rafting so instead of completing the next 9 rapids we opt for the 25-minute climb up to the tour bus.

On our way out I have taken the liberty to record the rafting adventure:

Start Point:	Big Eddy	Grade 0	Easy start.
Rapid One:	Boiling Pot	Grade 3	Got adrenalin pumping.
Rapid Four:	Morning Glory	Grade 4	Feel queasy already.
Rapid Five:	Stairway to Heaven	Grade 4	Nearly fell out of the raft.
Rapid Six:	Devil's Toilet Bowl	Grade 5	Tony's camera hit me in the face . . . .
Rapid Seven:	Gulliver's Travels	Grade 3	I got to steer the raft through.
Rapid Eight:	One and A Half	Grade 4	Tim fell out on the way down.
Rapid Nine:	Midnight Diner	Grade 5	Stomach makes its way into mouth.
Rapid Ten:	Commercial Suicide	Grade 4	Trevor and I saved dislodged rafters.
Rapid Eleven:	Jaws Of Death	Grade 5	Came face to face with God.

The sun has been blazing all day and, for the first time in years, I have been badly sunburnt. We meet Theresa and Martin in town and the crew drive out to the local elephant farm. Trevor and I book the night's entertainment and then meet the gang at the Victoria Falls Hotel for high tea. It is Zimbabwe's grandest hotel – a colonial legacy of architectural style and impeccable service. It was originally a small wood and corrugated iron shack to house the first tourists in 1905 who arrived by train. That small iron shack has certainly come a long way. Foreign tourists can indulge their rich-bwana fantasies here waited on by highly efficient black staff in starched white uniform and gloves.

It is the last bastion of the British influence in Victoria and we play it like any colonial scum. We take the complete mickey. The only real impact we make is by gobbling the free sandwiches.

Traditional dancing is the highlight of the evening, but we're all so knackered at this stage we wouldn't care if John Travolta appeared and heaved his pelvis. The last thing I remember is gobbling several pork sausages before I snored in tune with the rhinos.

It seems to be true test of adrenalin and power as we are whisked from our slumber to the heated tarmac of the airport – our third visit in two days. At 7.00am we meet up with Scruffy, Jim and Ian (native Zimbabweans) who take us up in the air for a tandem skydive. It is the best possible start to the day – we all feel completely knackered and the rush of adrenalin is welcome medicine.

Tony keeps his feet firmly on the ground while Tim and Nigel and strapped into the rear of the plane. The instructions are simple to follow: Stay relaxed, keep your head up and legs apart, and enjoy the ride. The free fall lasts 40 seconds but feels like 5 seconds. The effort in getting up is exhaustive, climbing to 10,000 feet, but the trip down takes a total of four and a half minutes. The thrill is beyond and above anything I've tried before, skydiving being the only remaining adrenalin sport on my list of 'Crazy Things to Do'. Today, in the morning heat of Northwest Zimbabwe, I complete my list.

Ian takes the plane down – almost vertically – which roughs up the crew a little. Best ride of the day and no-one there to capture it. We are met by 3 Kiwi girls at the bottom who are ready to take the plunge. I assure them it's worth the effort. It works out to cost approximately US$100 per leap. I have the trembling knees and bloodshot eyes as keep sake souvenirs.

We travel south to a small native village and meet a famous ex-freedom fighter who works as a traditional doctor. His youthful appearance belies his 53 years and he certainly has an interesting lifestory. 'Mpisi' (his nickname – it means hyena) could have held a high military position after the war but instead chose to return to the village in an attempt to improve the adverse living conditions of his people. He believes the 'civilising' influence of the colonials was counter-productive in many ways. His people have lost the ability to survive by using the old ways. Restoring the culture is of paramount importance to him. He believes his youthful appearance is due to an avoidance of Western food and medicine. He has lived off the resources the land can offer.

It is staggering to think that 70% of the Zimbabwean population still live this way. Their ways are simple but I've never seen so many smiles in one village.

A passing cart encounters a puncture so I help out. Mules pull the cart, as the driver and his wife begin a 20 kilometre trek to their home. Tim has been wearing shorts for the last few days and his knees have gone rosy-red with sunburn. He earns the nickname 'Strawberries'.

Back to Masuwe Lodge for lunch, and a chance meeting with Jonathan Ellway, the manager of Landela Lodges (the company in charge of our accommodation). He explains how the Lodges provide a unique experience, as they situate the accommodation so close to the action and the wildlife.

'After you spend the day spotting wildlife, you don't come in from the wild to an air-conned, high rise hotel room and flop down in front of the telly and watch CNN. Not here. You mix it with nature wherever you go.'

Another meal of meat. I would die for a salad.

Trevor takes us into town to visit the local resident witch doctor. I have my future told (quite bright by the sounds of things) and then play with the Marimba dancers. Theresa and I participate in the playing of the traditional wood chimes, and I accidentally break a musical instrument. They don't seem too worried, but I run away.

To the border of Zambia and Zimbabwe for the traditional bungy jump. Into No Man's Land where the bungy bridge is positioned high over the Zambesi River. Once the site of the world's tallest jump, the Vic Falls bungy is Kiwi-operated and owned – no real surprise there! Talk to Dave and Byron – two of the original crew responsible for driving from Johannesburg to set up this little operation. Two real characters who do their very best to wind me up before I jump. Several false countdowns and hard slaps on the back when I'm on the edge, before I take the plunge. The bungy gives you a free fall of about 100 metres before the cord takes the weight and then you are winched UP instead of down. Once conquering your fear of heights, you are then expected to put up with a second dizzying trip.

I had a High 8 handy cam attached to my hand but Nigel has forgotten to turn it on. The camera was aimed to film my face as I descended. We ponder the thought of a second jump but realise that time is too short. Our plane leaves in less than an hour and we are already late. He carries the 'Plonker of the Week' trophy the whole way.

To the airport and on board our Air Zimbabwe flight by 4.30pm. A peaceful flight to Hwange National Park takes only 30 minutes and we are served a fantastic chicken pita bread roll on board. Nigel has three. Fat bastard.

Hwange plays host to our second home Chokamella Lodge, which takes 2 hours to get to via bumpy and underdeveloped road. The journey is too uncomfortable to register any sleep but we make up for lost time when we arrive. Theresa falls asleep in the middle of dinner.

I almost had a heart attack this morning when I was putting on my sneakers. What I thought was a stuffed sock in the toe of my right No Fear trainer turned out to be a sleepy frog. My scream could be heard for miles. The frog's could be heard for several metres.

My bed was extremely comfortable but sleep was very short and full of disturbing dreams. The sleep-in ordered by our director is appreciated all round and we delay our departure further until 10.00am. Our drivers Eddie, Shepherd and Stephen entertain us with friendly banter on our way:

'You know man. This place never used to be called Hwange,' chimes Stephen.

'I s'pose the Poms called it something else did they?'

The journey takes roughly an hour and 20 minutes and on arrival Hwange National Park immediately offers plenty of wildlife. The park has a shifting population of around 4,000 elephants with a huge array of birds and insects. The highest concerntrations of game are in the dry-season (May–October) when the animals migrate to the waterholes. The best times for watching game are early morning and dusk but we strike a lucky time. We use 2 open-top vans to get ourselves around the park – early views of giraffes, baboons and zebras give us encouragement that we will capture plenty of footage today.

The sun is starting to penetrate my hardy skin. The heat is starting to bronze everybody and by 4.00pm we are sick of sunshine. Stopped for lunch at a constructed Viewing Platform, which overlooked the Park's main watering hole. Eddie delivers some superb safari advice over lunch:

'People come to Africa expecting animals on delivery. That's how we'd like it to be, but it never is. It's about putting away your watch and your preconceptions, relaxing and waiting.'

We have been lucky today, Tony has managed to shoot several Beta tapes of footage. We finish the day with a visit to a secluded Dam site where we encounter a wild bull elephant and I play rugby with one of its turds. Yum.

Finally made our way home (took several hours) and shot the magnificent sunset. Tea of chicken schnitzel and vegetables. By now, I wouldn't give a rat's arse about my fitness diet. I'm hungry and tired and want my bed. We sit up into the early hours viewing footage which is entertaining. Sleeping pills are not needed tonight.

Theresa and crew are up at the crack of dawn for a nature trek, which eventually ends in a torrential rainstorm, leaving them looking bedraggled and downtrodden when they return. Luckily the drops had started to fall as they were finishing so the main job has been done.

Our host, obviously sick of the Kiwis trying to phone home, has locked the office and refuses to let us make any calls. Our departure is delayed for ten minutes but eventually takes off bound for Chokamella.

The flight takes 30 minutes, the van from the airport to Lake Kariba takes 15 minutes and the boat ride to Chokamella Lodge takes an hour and 20 minutes.

We have visited some remote areas as part of this shoot but, on this occasion, we are hundreds of miles from civilisation. Only have time to quickly unpack and take the Lodge speedboat to a secluded spot on the Lake shoreline. Theresa and I are in festive mood (it must be those malaria pills) and decide to throw off our clothes in triumph of completing a huge day of making television.

As the boat carefully threads its way through the floating foliage, the spotlight occasionally highlights several pairs of beady orange eyes peering up from the water.

'Crocodiles' says Lawrence. I tighten my seatbelt.

'Heavens above. One hit and we're history'

Welcome to deepest Africa.

Woke to what sounded like a hippopotamus farting loudly outside my window. And it was. The burly animal issues a look of disgust and then wanders into the bush. A hasty breakfast and then a spot of game hunting with Lawrence and JJ in the speedboats. The sky darkens overhead, and a violent storm chops up the water. The sudden meteorological transformation takes us by surprise and we are drenched through in seconds. Two wind twisters appear only several hundred metres in front of us, which adds to this bizarre sight.

Almost as quickly, the sky clears and we reach the viewing harbour. We are treated to a full English breakfast that Lawrence has somehow packed into a tiny chilly bin, and we strip off our sodden t-shirts to dry as the hot sun bears down. Spotted hippos and elephants close to shore.

Back to base and a rushed packing job is done. This part of the journey is of paramount importance. If we miss one single connection today, we could be stuck in Africa for both Christmas and New Years so we need to be punctual for all departures – a factor often out of our control. We returned to camp in time to catch the midday boat to the airport, and then fly to Harare. A small drama unravels in the capital when the plane to Johannesburg starts rolling down the runway – without us. Bullshit red tape at the customs counter means we have been delayed.

We manage to stop the plane and jump aboard. 45 minutes later, we're in Johannesburg. Home for Christmas. Hooray!

CHAPTER 17 | CANADA

Day 121, Saturday 24th January

We don't clear Canadian customs for at least a quarter of an hour, but there is no shortage of typical Canadian hospitality – service with a smile. We have only encountered similar friendliness in Switzerland; it makes such an impression when you are greeted with open arms. A weary wander through the International Arrivals Reception, before being met by Nigel Carpenter (director) and Tom Ryan, our guide for the week.

Kerre Woodham has managed to find time in her hectic schedule to accompany me on this journey. Her radio show on 'Newstalk ZB' and successful cooking show 'Some Like It Hot!' on TV3 has guaranteed a full appointment page in her filofax. This week-long excursion, although arduous and difficult at times, will be a welcome rest from work. I am delighted to have her back on board. Kerre was the first presenter I worked with in television (London 1996). Her experience and professionalism was an influencing force in my early work, and I look forward to sharing her expertise again.

The weather is chilly and bleak – indeed, this city follows on from the heat of Northern Thailand, Zimbabwe and the United Arab Emirates as destinations for the crew – but it is refreshing and crisp. We cruise through downtown Vancouver and onto Comox Street, where the comfort of our hotel awaits us. I am ecstatic to find they have a gymnasium, and even more elated when I discover the sale of 'Twinkies' in the store nearby.

I travelled the length of the United States as a young backpacker in 1993, and almost lived on the cream-filled sponge desserts. Breakfast, lunch and dinner, my order was simple – Twinkies please! My taste buds are rewarded and I meet with Nigel to discuss the week's shoot:

'I don't know if we'll get a good show out of this place, mate.'

This is Nigel's catchphrase in almost every destination visited. He is a perfectionist who is only happy with 100% effort, and feels that Vancouver may not deliver any excitement. I take one look down the schedule (bridge swinging, snow-mobiling, snowboarding, skiing, motorbiking, mountain biking, playing rugby etc) and assure him that the programme looks fine.

The Coast Plaza Suite Hotel at Stanley Park overlooks the harbour and provides a few hours of rest before we meet at 2.00pm to discuss the week's plans.

Seeing that I am not needed for the afternoon I retire to my room to catch up on lost sleep. Coral Barrett, our researcher, calls in to say hi. She is returning to New Zealand this afternoon, and is genuinely sorry to be leaving. Her oversized travel bag lies testament to the shopping excellence of Canada. The researcher's job is indeed a worthwhile one.

For the first time in 21 destinations, I fall asleep almost immediately. The team travel out to shoot GV's (general vision) of the nightlife on Robson Street as well as some twilight pictures from The Lookout at Harbour Centre. I spend almost CDN$20 on taco chips and dip from Room Service, after I wake at midnight.

The bellboy delivers the meal and waits patiently for his tip. 15% is the acceptable rate of tipping for waiting and service, with some restaurants and hotels including the appreciation fee in the bill. It is a concept that I struggled to adopt when visiting the United States, but accepted it was often the primary source of income for most workers and gave generously.

A quick breakfast of bagels and coffee (is this New York?) and we travel north to the bottom of Grouse Mountain and stop at the Capilano Suspension Bridge. Standing at 250ft in height and 430ft in length, it is listed in the Guinness Book of World Records as the longest-highest suspension bridge in the world. Kerre is scared to death of heights, which makes the 'crossing' all the more exciting.

'You've seen Indiana Jones, haven't you?' I giggle.

'Don't even think about it!' she screams.

The panoramic view of the mountain is staggering, its exquisite beauty rivalling anything our country has to offer, but the chilly mountain air sneaks up on us without warning and after only 20 minutes, Kerre and I are shivering. Technical problems with the audio equipment further extend our discomfort.

We head further north towards Grouse Mountain and pass the film set for *X-Files* on the way. Oddly enough Vancouver supplies the backdrop for numerous television productions – *X-Files, Millennium, Twilight Zone* and occasional episodes of *The Outer Limits*. The lowly mist and shadowy landscape simply ooze a haunting mysticism.

We detour through Stanley Park, which is swarming with thousands of joggers and rollerbladers, who use the park's circular design to shed those unneeded kilograms. With the exception of Wellington's Oriental Parade and Auckland's Mission Bay, I have never seen such a throng of people who are braving the 9-degree temperatures to enjoy their outdoor pursuits. A mountain bike is hired and muddy trails are annihilated by my frantic pedaling.

Delivering my lines for camera is often easier when I am trying to negotiate difficult elements; tandem, helicopter, bungy – you name it, I've done it. My brief is simple and straightforward: I simply 'bunny-hop' over a small hill, negotiate my way through a small gap in the trees and accelerate round a sharp bend. Dress rehearsal is problem-free, but sadly on the second run the back tyre slips on an obscure rock and . . . BAMMM! The bike stops. I don't.

I collapse into a tangle of spokes and limbs as man becomes one with machine. My right hand is forced underneath the bike, which promotes an instantaneous pain in my thumb. A quick assessment is made of the damage. The thumb looks bruised and sore, the skin has been taken off the top, and it quickly stiffens.

'Do you want to carry on?' my director asks.

'Yep.'

'Are you sure?'

'Yeah, yeah. I've broken it before.'

'Think of the bigger picture, mate. Stop if you need to.'

It's a loaded statement. Even though, my thumb is obviously damaged there is no question of resting up. Our schedule is engaging enough without the need for additional holdups. I compromise my position:

'Nigel, I'll get it checked tonight before we go out.'

'Well, it's your call!'

Stop for lunch: burgers and fries. A game of rugby is the next thing on the agenda, but I insist to Nigel that I will need the thumb taped. There are two lumps that have formed on the underside of the thumb which is worrying me. Nigel asks me whether I wish to carry on. It's a bit of a catch-22 situation. If I pull the pin, the shoot is in danger of collapsing into a complete mess. If I choose to carry on regardless, I risk further personal injury and possible permanent damage.

I choose the latter.

The Evergreen Rugby Club has 4 teams but only the older, hardier gents are out today. The Over 40's are a mixture of native Vancouverites with a mild sprinkling of Kiwis and Poms. A relaxed game of touch provides an ideal opportunity to mingle with the locals. I thoroughly enjoy the exercise and even score a few tries. On-field rugby antics are the same worldwide:

'Pass. Pass. Pass. Pass the bloody ball, ya fat Irish bastard.'

'I would if you could keep up.'

'Stop yakking and get on with it, lads.'

'Kiwi wanker.'

Unfortunately, we are unable to stay for the after-match beers but are grateful for their time. I have strapped my thumb with X54 medical tape, but it aches with pain. I'm starting to get a little annoyed that I have to run around in mud for a few seconds of TV coverage.

Grouse Mountain provides limited skiing and snowboard runs but is still a popular tourist attraction because of the expansive view of the city and its accessibility. To get to the top, the Gondola ride takes 15 minutes – another opportunity for scaring Kerre. She's absolutely petrified of heights and today has hardly been therapeutic. The chill is pretty terrifying when we reach the summit so filming is quick.

The last Sunday of January is significant in sporting circles for one particular reason. The whole of North America stops in its tracks to watch the SuperBowl. Expect, it seems, visiting New Zealand film crews. Because there is such value in a day's filming, the SuperBowl sits low on our list of priorities. Tom is a Green Bay fan and, although he is keen to watch, he pretends he doesn't care.

We are due to go to Bubalu's Smoke and Tapas Lounge but Tom and I pop into St. Paul's Accident and Emergency Hospital to get my thumb checked. Some consolation in the fact that there is a live sports broadcast in the waiting lounge.

An hour's wait and an x-ray later, Doctor Clive Barrington informs that the thumb is broken in several places (Much of a surprise to all of us, best bets were on 'heavily bruised'.) and will take six weeks to heal. Nigel's shock is laced with a feeling of guilt. But he quickly orders that I take my heavy dosage of painkillers and retire for the evening. The smile on Tom's face (having watched the whole game at the hospital) lights up the night.

Checkout. Early start and on the 'Caribou Prospector' BC Rail Train to Whistler resort by 6.30am. The scenic ride takes all of 2 hours and winds its way up the coast line and into the fabulous Blackcomb Mountain range. Because it is so early, the train staff serve a breakfast of omelette and waffles, washed down with dashings of coffee and orange juice.

Tony and Tom have the unenviable task of chasing the train in the tourist van. This involves taking shots as the 'Caribou' approaches, packing up the camera and tripod, and then racing ahead for another shot. This carries on for a couple of hours before we disembark and join forces at the Whistler Resort. The train drivers, Ollie and Dan, give us a friendly wave and chug off into the distance.

Once booked into the Chateau Whistler, we all trudge off to the Blackcomb Day Lodge to collect ski-gear. This takes about an hour, and following that we head up ski-lift Four to meet our ski-instructor for the afternoon's lesson. Ralph is Canadian and is only too happy to instruct Kerre as part of the film shoot.

Tony had often explained the necessity of being able to ski to work as a cameraman, or even sound tech, and this becomes immediately obvious. Watching him and Matt trail Kerre and Ralph down the mountain with no poles and kilos of equipment is admirable. Because of my thumb, I am only able to walk down the mountain carrying gear; I am not an able enough skier to go without poles.

Today is Australia Day so the multitude of Australians who work at Whistler Resort (almost 50% of all manual workers) are in celebratory mood. A huge snow sculpture of Skippy the Kangaroo overlooks the Olympic Station. The temptation to kick its head off is great but for sake of international diplomacy, I refrain.

The day in the snow has left everybody weary and, although we intended to spend the evening at the Australia Day celebrations at Merlin's, Nigel thinks that the day has been long enough.

Kerre has the ultimate wake-up this morning. A two-hour treatment at the Health Spa involves a face-pack, steam bath and massage, and is conducted for the purpose of filming. Lucky cow.

At 11.00am, Tom takes us to the Canadian Snowmobile Adventures camp where our instructors Randy and Frenchie meet and greet. Frenchie is from Quebec but has worked here for several months., while Randy is the old veteran. He talks of the numerous TV stars he has entertained.

'We had a *Baywatch* beauty here last year,' he beams, producing a framed photograph.

Our jaws drop at the site of Gena Lee Nolan, the blonde bombshell from the award-winning TV show. Unfortunately, she is fully clothed.

'She sure was fun!'

'You haven't met Kerre yet.'

Frenchie has control of his ski-doo like Schumacher has of his Formula One motorcar, and we all trail our way through Blackcomb Mountain at breakneck speed. His daredevil antics cause me to fall off the snow-mobile several times. I land on my thumb on both occasions, sending a white shot of pain through my whole arm. This brings tears to my eyes.

'Why don't you hold on tighter?'

'I've only got one arm!'

'What are you? A poof?'

'No. Just French.'

I conduct an interview with Frenchie, sitting atop our ski-doo, and insist that he replies in his native tongue. It is an interview with a difference. Just the sort of Destination Planet Earth moment that we're after. The only conversation I've ever had, where I haven't understood a word.

Kerre has never driven a ski-doo before, but after only a few minutes she is a pro. We stop on several occasions to take in the breathtaking view – the alpine scenery is quite staggering. Pine trees litter the hills in abundance, powdered snow resting gently on the branches – like icing on a Christmas cake; the only audible sound comes from the mechanical clunking of the gondolas in the distance. We knock off several shots, the opening to the show and then head down the mountain.

As a considerable youngster on this show, I have to endure visits to museums and landscapes (boring!). Finally, tonight I get the opportunity to indulge in a truly childish activity. Mountain World is an adult entertainment (no, not that sort!) centre, which provides the older generation with a choice of high-tech video games in the comfort of a multi-purpose complex with bar and restaurant.

The eyeballs seem to widen as various racing video games appear from the shadowy depths. 'Daytona 500', ' Olympic Downhill' and 'Formula One' take up much of the evening and our hosts, Alasdair Douglas and Glenn Fawcett, provide free pizza and beverages once we've exhausted our 'testosterone' reserves. Tony becomes racing champion. I bring in the bronze.

Kerre has tried to contact us from her room in the chateau, but the message has been lost in the excitement. While we've been playing and eating, she has been waiting in the foyer for our return. She's not pleased and rightly so.

There has been much debate as to how we incorporate my broken thumb into the show.

It has been decided that we should fake a doctor's examination, and place it at the top of Part One so that viewers won't become confused when they see the cast. Although it may sound trivial, any inconsistencies will be quickly realised. We use a room in the Health Club, and borrow one of the staff members to pretend to analyse my x-ray.

At 10.30pm we call it quits. Matt is hot and tired. It has been another long day.

The Whistler Mountain Public Relations Manager, Susan Darch, has insisted that I accompany the Ski Patrol on their early inspection rounds. This happens every morning in the form of Avalanche Control, which involves surveying the unstable snowfields, organising team rallies and throwing explosive mortars – cool! Coincidentally this morning's team leader is a New Zealander who has worked on the mountain for several months on the Avalanche Control Squad. Richard is from Queenstown, which explains his love of skiing and snow.

We take several Gondola trips to reach to the top of Blackcomb Mountain – a monstrous 2,850 metres high – while the weather deteriorates dramatically. The snow has turned into sleet, the winds wail through at high speed and standing upright becomes a real challenge. It is suggested that Richard and I conduct the interview before we get blown off the mountain and descend as quickly as possible. I have visions of getting trapped for days.

Unfortunately, we are too late and the weather causes the closure of the top cable car. This means that the crew have to ski 5 miles to the bottom, while Nigel and I are ski-dooed down the mountain with all the gear. Images of 'last minute James Bond-like escapes' come to mind but, like most situations we get ourselves into, it all turns out rosy.

We pack quickly and head off to Vancouver. On the way Tom rings ahead to McDonald's and we collect a quick snack on the road – such is the nature of our schedule – and arrive at Vancouver's Coal Harbour by midday.

All five of us, minus Tom who must take the ferry with the equipment, squeeze into a Harbour Seaplane (a boat plane) and take the 35-minute flight to Vancouver Island. The picture postcard view is worth the effort as we head up Active Pass, over the Gulf Isles and over the city of Victoria, and then cruise into the harbour. Zollie is our pilot and proves to be outstanding talent for the camera, and he even lets me pilot the plane – quite a brave thing to do, given that I am a hopeless driver. My thrill is evident as I 'whoop' and 'scream'.

We transfer to Laurel Point Inn and watch the day's rushes in Nigel's suite. The alcohol in his fridge disappears in seconds and I order room service orange juice – a real steal at CDN$25 a jug. In an effort to sleep I watch the porn channel. My chosen movie is *Nasty Nymphos* but I've already seen it. This particular version is edited.

This morning starts at 9.00am, and a two hour journey to Nanaimo which takes us past Goldstream Park, The Malahat Look-out, Cobble Hill (Wine and Ciderworks), Chemainus and Duncan (home of the largest hockey stick in the world) so there's plenty to look at.

At lunchtime, we arrive at The Nanaimo Bungy Zone and Adrenalin Centre and are greeted by the manager, another Kiwi, Fiona Cox-Jansen. There is an annual Naked Weekend run at Nanaimo for crazy people who are keen to bungy in the buff. Nigel has asked whether I would be keen or not. Stupid question. I undress.

Because we've covered bungy in previous shows, we decide it may be better to try the bridge swing. Fiona informs me that no-one has ever tried the swing without any clothes before:

'What? So we're the first?'

'Yep.'

'Why? Surely people who bungy in the nude would find it easy to swing?'

'Have a look at your harness.' she points out.

It dangles over the counter, ready for inspection. It's obvious the crotch area will be exposed to intense pressure during the downward moment, and I wince with the anticipation of the discomfort.

'Perhaps you should wear ya undies mate.'

Determined to be the first 'proper' naked swinger, I have insisted that I cover my private parts with a sock and some gaffer tape, so the 'taping' operation takes place in the centre toilets. My pubic hair takes a real battering in my pathetic attempts to hide my manhood behind the frail nylon fabric of an airplane sock.

The result is some Frankenstein-type g-string, which reduces everybody to tears. Laughter that is, not anguish.

The temperature has dropped considerably, and I start to feel the chill of the morning as I disrobe for my swing. My instructor Kevin, who seems concerned about my state of dress, harnesses me in. The tension on the swing is provided by the overhead cable and the immediate pull is evident as the platform is dropped and I freefall for about 40 metres before arcing into a mammoth swing.

I am lowered into a passing speedboat and begin the steady climb to the top. I have been exposed to the open air for just over 5 minutes and I start to shiver uncontrollably. Kerre meets me at the top with a jacket in an attempt to slowly warm-up. My thumb is throbbing and I feel completely out of my 'comfort' zone. It's times like these which I wish the viewing public could see the work that goes in behind the scenes. Glamorous job this.

I take the plunge twice more (for different camera angles) and then holler for assistance in 'disrobing'. Kerre gets to pull off my protective sock. The local wildlife is introduced to the distressing call of 'The Screaming Maori'. A nasty storm front is due to settle in, resulting in the next part of our programme having to be cancelled. The Coastline Motorbike Club were due to bring out a couple of Harley Davidson bikes for Kerre to ride but the road conditions are considered too treacherous to negotiate.

As a result the trip back to Victoria is made immediately. Tom was raised in this province and proudly points out the significant landmarks, along with family trivia on the journey:

'You see this running track? My older brother ran 9.7 seconds for the 100 yards on the day of the moon landing. And that road? We lived there, next to a Native Reserve area.'

Even at the local KFC restaurant, he fires an assault on the local workers:

'Hey, what high school did you guys go to? Oh, really?

You probably know my brother? Jimmy Ryan? He was a headmaster there.'

The view from the balcony of Nigel's hotel room – occupied earlier in the year by Sharon Stone – overlooks downtown Victoria so we position the camera to record the early evening spectacle. The city seems to become more animated at nightfall, and the crew decide to capitalise on its beauty by eating out at a local restaurant.

I am ordered by management to sit in the Jacuzzi in an effort to warm up. My bones are still quaking with the chill of this morning, and the tepid bath of bubbles soon turns me into a bleedin' prune. At about 7.15pm, Donna from reception delivers a facsimile recently arrived from New Zealand from a former work colleague. It contains a number of scandalous allegations in a direct attack on my professionalism and ability as a presenter. The crew is shocked and appalled at this completely unwarranted assault and several phone calls to executives are made. The individual concerned has worked on 'Destination Planet Earth' before and fuelled debate ensues as to the reasons for this bizarre and completely unexpected communication.

The mood darkens over the crew, and the evening becomes one of analysis instead of reflection on another successful day.

The Harleys arrive at 9.00am, thankfully able to shift their appointment to this morning, and we drive around the country areas. I sit and ride with Jackie Morrow who together with husband Barry own the Coastline Motorcycle Company and follow Kerre.

We are pushed for time today, and once finished filming we line the van at Swartz Bay to catch the 11.00am BC Ferry. We are two minutes too late and need to wait for a couple of hours to get the next one. This proves to be a small blessing in disguise, and it gives the crew the opportunity to visit an old English-style pub, have a game of darts (I beat Tom with my left hand) and a massive nosh-up.

The BC Ferry trip takes a couple of hours to Tsawwassen, but the view is worthwhile. Kerre and I steal a few minutes snooze before we disembark and head to the centre of Vancouver. Tom's wife Mika and son Tyler meet us in the city centre and we all head to the Yaletown Brewing

Company for a quick pepperoni pizza and then catch the tram to the General Motors Place.

The sports announcer broadcasts over the loudspeaker:

'Tonight's featured game is the National League Ice Hockey clash between the Vancouver Canucks and New Jersey Devils. Let's get ready for the coolest game on ice.'

The stadium is grandiose and the local crowd gradually swells to leave no empty seats. The marketing and promotions for American professional sports leagues are top notch and during the game we are entertained by pop bands, dance music, bass chants, parachute prizes, lucky seat numbers and the $50,000 ice hockey shot – all extremely well organised entertainment.

The game itself is a tight battle, with the Canucks leading with only 40 seconds to go. The 2-1 scoreline cushion the Canadians have built looks in danger until the home team steals the puck and scores on fulltime. The crowd goes berserk and we retire happy that we've collected some outstanding footage.

Another tight fit as we pack the van and head to the airport to collect some pickup shots of the boat plane that we rode earlier in the week. Our check-in time for international departure is midday but we don't arrive until 12.30pm, and there is general fear that we will miss out on business class. No chance.

It's time to go home.